Baxter's Guide

Biographical Sources in the India Office Records

Ian A Baxter

3rd Edition

Families In British India Society   In association with The British Library

The Families in British India Society (FIBIS) is a registered charity (No.1072403) formed in November 1998 to support persons seeking to study their ancestors' lives in India.
FIBIS website: www.fibis.org

Cover photo
A group of Europeans riding on elephants, 1890s (photographer: J C Townshend).
A note on the original states: "*A week later the middle elephant killed his mahut*"
By permission of The British Library, Photo 1056/(50)

Note
Sources which are available on the open shelves at The British Library are indicated by an asterisk

Published by the Families in British India Society
In association with The British Library

British Library Cataloguing in Publication Data
A catalogue record for this book is available from The British Library

ISBN 0-9547-116-0-2

Design for cover, map and other additional material for the 3rd Edition by Anne Kelsall

Typeset and printed in Great Britain by Athenaeum Press, Gateshead

Contents

Foreword

This book, now generally referred to as 'Baxter's Guide', has become an essential reference work for all who research the history of their families who served in India. Although modest in size, it brings together a clear set of references to the enormous number of biographical sources scattered amongst the 15 km of shelves of the India Office Records.

The Families in British India Society (FIBIS) was formed in November 1998 to provide help and advice to individuals wishing to research their family history and the social and historical background of their ancestors' lives in India from the founding of the East India Company in 1600 until the present day.

The relevance of the Guide to our Society's purpose is self-evident. Its first two editions sold out relatively quickly and the British Library has now decided that its information will largely be made available on the Library's website. However, we believe that, given the burgeoning interest in pursuing family history in India and South Asia, and for ease of reference, many new researchers would still welcome the chance to obtain the Guide in convenient book form. Accordingly, the British Library has kindly given permission to the Families in British India Society to undertake a new edition, for which we express our gratitude.

This third edition of the Guide has been augmented by FIBIS in association with its author, Ian Baxter, to include his Glossary of terms used in the administration of British India. The opportunity has also been taken to include the India Office Records note on the three geographical areas for 'Ecclesiastical Returns' – those records of baptisms, marriages and burials so fundamental to family history research. The map illustrating these areas and other major administrative divisions of British India has been redrawn by Anne Kelsall, one of our members, and appears on the back cover. We are grateful to the British Library for permission to include this additional material.

It is appropriate to remark that an increasing number of transcriptions and indexes of ecclesiastical and other records, both in the India Office Records and elsewhere, are being created. Some are available on the internet, and FIBIS is continuously developing its own website (www.fibis.org) to provide both its own databases, and links to others, which are relevant to India-related biographical research. It is also worth noting that researchers needing assistance with their India-related enquiries may find it by joining the India List, a forum for exchange of information (http://lists.rootsweb.com/index/intl/IND/INDIA.html); and of course they will also find it worthwhile to join FIBIS which offers help to its members with their family history research.

Peter Bailey
Chairman,
Families in British India Society

February 2004

Introduction to the Third Edition

Biographical sources are scattered throughout the India Office Records, but this *Guide* indicates those of primary importance to family history researchers. It is arranged according to categories of persons to enable researchers, armed only with a basic occupational description and a date, to pursue further information on the individual in whom they are interested. But besides sources specific to a particular category of persons, some are potentially relevant whatever an individual's occupation. Page 1 lists a number of such published sources, and there are two very important record series of general relevance.

Firstly, there are the Ecclesiastical Returns (IOR series N) of baptisms/births, marriages, and burials/deaths for British India and related territories, 1698-1947, with a very few post-independence entries. This is the most important source of general biographical information in the India Office Records. They relate mainly to European and Eurasian Christians and are about 80% complete for those categories. However, the percentage for Roman Catholic returns is much lower. The series also contains a very small number of post-independence returns, 1948-1963. The returns are filed and indexed under three large geo-political divisions: Bengal, Madras and Bombay. In this context the term 'Bengal' covers not only Bengal proper, but also the whole of northern India from Burma in the east to Baluchistan in the west, as well as (until 1867) the Straits Settlements (Singapore, Penang, Malacca); the term 'Madras' covers eastern and southern peninsular India, and the term 'Bombay' western peninsular India, Sind and Aden. After the creation of the Burma Office in 1937 returns for Burma were kept separately from the Bengal returns and are separately indexed. For more detailed information on the N series and directions as to its use, see the booklet entitled 'Ecclesiastical Returns' available free at the British Library. The three main series for Bengal (N/1), Madras (N/2) and Bombay (N/3) have been microfilmed, including the indexes (Z/N/-), and are searchable not only at the British Library but also at the Family History Centres of the Church of Jesus Christ of the Latter Day Saints, along with microfilms of many other sources cited in this *Guide*. Although the indexes to the Registrar marriages (Z/N/11) have also been filmed, the actual records (N/11) are currently not available outside the India Office Records. Users at the India Office Records may find it helpful to begin with the *General Biographical Index*, a card index containing more than a quarter of a million entries giving details of many (though by no means all) of the baptisms, marriages and burials in India, and occasional information from other sources.

Also important as a source of biographical information are the series of wills, administrations, inventories and estate accounts for persons (mainly Europeans and Eurasians) dying in British India and related territories, 1618-1948. These comprise both a general series covering all categories of persons both official and non-official, and a military series, 1792-1948, relating to European officers and other ranks of the East India Company/Indian Army. Testamentary records prior to *c*1775 are to be found mainly in the Mayor's Court Proceedings (see IOR/P series), and after that date mainly in the records of the Accountant-General's Department (IOR/L/AG/34). Indexes to the general series are available in the Reading Room, as is a 'Guide to Wills' which includes a full list. A great many of these records have been filmed and are available through Family History Centres.

One disappointment is that the records of the Indian Decennial Census, 1871 *et seq* (IOR/V/15) do not, unlike the UK Census, provide personal particulars of individual inhabitants.

Finally, I should like to express my gratitude to FIBIS for bringing this *Guide* back into print.

Ian A Baxter

General Sources

While it may appear obvious to point out that enquirers should consult biographical dictionaries and similar works before proceeding to more specific sources of information, this stage is frequently omitted.

The main general reference works available in the Catalogue Hall are as follows:

The dictionary of national biography . . . from the earliest times to 1900, 22 vols (London, 1963–64 rep), with *Supplements 1901–1970*, 7 vols (London, 1927–81) and *Corrections and additions* (Boston, 1966)

Modern English biography, ed Frederic Boase, 6 vols (London, 1965), covers people who died between 1851 and 1900

Who was who, 8 vols, 1897–1980 (London, 1962–81) and the current issue of *Who's who Office-holders in modern Britain*, comp John Christopher Sainty (London, 1972–)

Works covering India include:

Dictionary of Indian biography, Charles Edward Buckland (London, 1906), includes people still alive at the time of compilation

The Indian biographical dictionary, C. Hayavadana Rao (Madras, 1915), deals with distinguished Europeans and Asians still alive in 1915

An oriental biographical dictionary, Thomas William Beale (London, 1894), includes many names from the Indian medieval period

Annals of the Oriental Club 1824–1858, ed Stephen Wheeler (London, 1925), gives brief sketches of members, many of them Directors or ex-India servants

Dictionary of national biography, ed S. P. Sen, 4 vols (Calcutta, 1972–74), covers distinguished Asians, living and dead, in undivided India from the eighteenth century to 1947

The national biographical dictionary of India, Jagdish Saran Sharma (New Delhi, 1972)

Who's who in India, with *1st & 2nd supplements*, (Lucknow, 1911–14)

Indian who's who (Bombay 1937–38)

Who's who in India, Burma and Ceylon (Bombay 1940–41)

Who's who in India, ed Hemraj Kothari (Calcutta 1973)

India who's who, current issue

Encyclopaedia of India's struggle for freedom, Jagdish Saran Sharma (New Delhi, 1971)

Who's who of Indian martyrs, ed Pran Nath Chopra (New Delhi, 1969–73), covers the Mutiny 1857–59 and the Independence Movement 1885–1947

Distinguished teachers in India, ed Raj Khosla (New Delhi, 1968)

Eminent Mussalmans (Madras, c1925)

Biographical encyclopaedia of Pakistan (Lahore, 1970)

Scientists and technologists of Pakistan (Karachi, 1966)

Historical and political who's who of Afghanistan, Ludwig Adamec (Graz, 1975)

There are also a number of calendars and transcripts of the early records, whose indexes are invaluable for research on seventeenth century individuals:

Calendar of State Papers, Colonial Series, East Indies . . . 1513–1634, ed William Noel Sainsbury, 5 vols (London, 1862–92)

A calendar of the Court Minutes etc of the East India Company 1635–1679, ed Ethel Bruce Sainsbury, 11 vols (Oxford, 1907–38)

Letters received by the East India Company from its servants in the East 1602–1617, ed Frederick Charles Danvers & William Foster, 6 vols (London, 1896–1902)

The English factories in India 1618–1684, ed William Foster & Charles Fawcett, 17 vols (Oxford, 1906–55)

Directors of the East India Company 1600–1858 (1874)

Lists of Directors 1600–1858 appear in IOR: H/764

A list (not always accurate) of Directors 1708–1858, and of Chairmen and Deputy-Chairmen 1714–1858, is printed in *Record of services of Madras civilians 1741–1858*, Charles Campbell Prinsep (London, 1885)

Lists of Directors are given in the *Bengal calendar* for 1790, the *East India register* 1800–58, and the *Asiatic journal* 1816–45 IOL: ST 76, which includes addresses

'Alphabetical list of Directors of the East India Company 1758–1858', Cyril Henry & D Philips, *Journal of the Royal Asiatic Society*, 1941, Pt 4, pp 325–36, IOL: ST 447, records against each name the years served as Director, Deputy-Chairman or Chairman

Some Directors were former servants of the Company – *see* pp 10, 15, 38

The history of Parliament – the House of Commons 1715–1754, ed Romney Sedgwick; *1754–1790*, ed Lewis Namier & John Brooke; *1790–1820*, ed R. G. Thorne (London 1964–86), is useful for Directors who were also Members of Parliament or related to members

All Directors were Company stockholders – *see* p 5

For the administrative records of the Court of Directors *see* Court Minutes IOR: B, General Committees and Offices IOR: D, General Correspondence IOR: E and L/AG/44

See also 'The Directors of the East India Company, 1754–1790' by James Gordon Parker. University of Edinburgh. Ph.D. thesis, 1977. Contains full biographical notes on all those who served as Directors between 1754 and 1790, inclusive, with numerous references to official records/private papers. The IOR holds a typescript copy

Members of the Board of Commissioners for the Affairs of India (Board of Control) and their Staff 1784–1858

A list of the Presidents of the Board of Control 1784–1858 appears in *Record of services of Madras civilians 1741–1858,* Charles Campbell Prinsep (London, 1885)

A list of the Commissioners is given in the *Bengal calendar* for 1790. The Commissioners and their staff, including clerks, messengers, and, from 1819, porters, are recorded in the *East India register* 1800–58

For Letters Patent appointing the Commissioners 1790–1853, *see* IOR: 0/1/412–56

For records of the payment of salaries to the Board of Control staff 1785–1858, see IOR: L/AG/43/1/1–8

For records of the payment of pensions to retired staff *see* IOR: L/AG/21/6

The administrative records of the Board of Control are in IOR: F, and *see also* Letters between the Board and the Court of Directors in IOR: E/2

Career details of Board of Control staff 1784–1858 (ie appointments, transfers, promotions, retirements) are to be found in L/AG/43/2/1–3. *See* also Board of Control Minutes, F/1/1–7 (1785–1858) which, from 1816 onwards, are devoted entirely to staff matters. Both these series are indexed

Members of the Council of India 1858–1937, and of the Board of Advisers to The Secretary of State for India and Burma 1937–1948

A list of the members of the Council of India 1858–1937, and of its successor the Board of Advisers 1937–48, appears in the *Supplement* to the *India Office and Burma Office list 1947*

Lists of members of the Council appear in the *East India register* 1858–60, the *Indian Army and Civil Service list* 1861–76, the *India list* 1877–1906, and the *India Office list* 1907–37. Advisers are recorded in the *India and Burma Office list* 1938–47. Short records of service of members of the Council are given in the *India Office list* from 1886 and of the Board in the *India and Burma Office list* from 1938

Biographical details of members of the Council and of the Advisers are recorded in annual India Office Establishment Lists from 1907, IOR: L/AG/30/18/24–68, and in India Office Establishment Papers, IOR: L/AG/30/22

Members of the Council and the Board were often former servants of the East India Company, the India Office or the Burma Office – *see* pp 6, 10, 15, 23

For the administrative records of the Council and the Board *see* IOR: C

East India Company Stockholders 1600–1874

For records of seventeenth century stockholders
see IOR: L/AG/14/2–3 and also lists in IOR: H/1
(1631–42, 1675, 1691 & 1693), H/2 (1694–96 &
1699), H/3 (1701–03 & 1707), L/AG/1/10/1
(1669), L/AG/1/10/2 (1688), A/53 & 54B (1698),
and MSS Eur D 774 (1690). Court Minutes, IOR:
B, record all transfers of shares down to 1694

The stock ledgers of the United East India
Company 1709–1849, IOR: L/AG/14/5/1–47, are
alphabetically arranged by names of
stockholders, recording each purchase and sale,
and addresses are also given. Stock ledgers from
Mar 1849 are held by the Archive Section of the
Bank of England, Threadneedle St, London
EC2R 8AH

There are separate printed *lists of stockholders
with voting rights (ie possessing at least £1000 of
stock) for 8 Apr 1795 & 9 Apr 1806.
Alphabetically arranged, they record the number
of votes and the address of each stockholder.
The same information appears twice yearly in the
East India register from 1822 to 1858

For other records relating to stocks and bonds
1700–1874 *see* the series IOR: L/AG/14/4–7 &
L/AG/15. IOR: L/AG/14/7/1 is a useful record of
the actual as opposed to the nominal selling price
of East India stocks and bonds on each day from
1 Oct 1732 to 28 Feb 1838

For stockholders 1858–74 *see* the series L/AG/44

Home Civil Servants of The East India Company 1600–1858, The India Office 1858–1947, and The Burma Office 1937–1948

Records of home staff appointments can be found in Court Minutes IOR: B, Committee of Correspondence records IOR: D, and Minutes and correspondence of the Finance and Home Committee 1834–59 IOR: L/F/1–2. Appointments to the Auditor's Department appear in the series Auditors' References 1740–1835 IOR: D/147–252. There is also a series of bonds and agreements for the home establishment 1788–1860, IOR: O/1/197–206 index IOR: Z/0/1/6, which give dates of appointment and the names and addresses of sureties

Occasional lists of home staff c1660–1717 appear in Court Minutes IOR: B. IOR: H/67 lists home staff at various dates 1710–93 and records their salaries and gratuities. IOR: H/362 records home staff in 1785 with a statement of salaries and duties

The salary books of established home staff Mar 1760–Sep 1860, IOR: L/AG/9/4/13–20 & L/AG/19/2/1–10, give complete lists of staff for each quarter of a year, including warehousemen, porters etc. There are also salary books for non-established staff (temporaries, messengers etc) 1810–58, IOR: L/AG/19/3/1–7

Lists of home staff appear twice yearly in the *East India register* 1800–58

For pensions paid to retired home staff from 1758 *see* the series IOR: L/AG/9/4 & 21/1, which sometimes give addresses

There are numerous compilations covering all grades of home staff in IOR: L/AG/30, particularly IOR: L/AG/30/12, which contains notes on the careers of home staff c1834–58

Home staff contributed to the Regular Widows' or Elders' Widows' Funds, set up in 1816 and closed to new subscribers in 1862. For the administrative records of these funds, which contain a great deal of family information, *see* IOR: L/AG/23/3A. Payment books 1817–1966,

which sometimes give addresses, are in IOR: L/AG/21/23

INDIA OFFICE 1858–1947 AND BURMA OFFICE 1937–1948

Lists of home establishment staff, including porters and messengers, appear in the *East India register* 1858–60, the *Indian Army and Civil Service list* 1861–76, the *India list* 1877–1906, the *India Office list* 1907–37 and the *India and Burma Office list* 1938–47. Brief records of service of professional home civil servants appear in the *India Office list* from 1886

Service statements of members of the permanent home establishment 1858–85 appear in IOR: L/AG/30/17/2–3 – dates of birth are given occasionally in 17/2 and for most entries in 17/3

The annual India Office Establishment Lists Jan 1884–Apr 1948, IOR: V/6/248–76, give dates of birth, dates of appointment, promotions and salaries. Burma Office staff are included from 1938

More detailed information on India Office personnel can be found in Home Establishment Papers 1884–85 & 1890–1951, IOR: L/AG/30/22/15 & 21–60 and L/S & G/8

There are also personal files maintained by the Salaries Section of the Accountant General's Department 1921–c1960, IOR: L/AG/29/3/1–34, and *see* Establishment Officer's personal files c1920–c1970 in IOR: L/S & G/9

For salary books of established and non-established home staff 1858–1951 *see* IOR: L/AG/19/2/10–43 & L/AG/19/3/8–51

For pensions paid to retired home staff 1858–1964 *see* the series IOR: L/AG/21/1, which sometimes gives addresses

Home staff contributed to the India Office Provident Fund, established in 1877 and closed to new subscribers in 1885. IOR: L/AG/23/4/2 is a complete family register of subscribers from 1877, giving dates of birth, marriage and death of subscriber, wife's dates of birth and death, children's dates of birth etc. For pension payment books of the Provident Fund 1880–1967, which sometimes give addresses, *see* the series IOR: L/AG/21/24

East India College (Haileybury), Addiscombe Military Seminary, Pembroke House and Ealing Lunatic Asylum, and The Royal Indian Engineering College (Cooper's Hill)

The records of the East India College Haileybury and other institutions, Anthony Farrington (London, 1976)

EAST INDIA COLLEGE, HERTFORD 1806–1809, HAILEYBURY 1809–1857

Memorials of old Haileybury College, Frederick Charles Danvers &others (London 1894), contains biographical notes on staff and students

For the administrative records of the College *see* the series IOR: J

Staff appointments are recorded in Court Minutes IOR: B, Committee of College Minutes 1804–34 IOR: J/2/1–12, Proceedings of the Court of Directors relating to Haileybury 1804–21 IOR: J/3/1–3, and Minutes and correspondence of the Finance and Home Committee 1834–59 IOR: L/F/1–2

Lists of the College staff appear twice-yearly in the *East India register* 1806–57

There are notes on members of the Haileybury staff in IOR: L/AG/30/6 (1817, 1827) and L/AG/30/12/ (1834–58)

Records of salary payments to the Haileybury staff 1830–51 are in the series IOR: L/AG/45/1/1. For pensions paid to retired members of staff *see* the series IOR: L/AG/9/4 & L/AG/21/6

ADDISCOMBE MILITARY SEMINARY 1809–1861

Addiscombe: its heroes and men of note, Henry Meredith Vibart (London 1894)

For administrative records and records of staff and students see IOR: L/MIL/1/9–80 & L/MIL/9/333–57

Staff appointments are recorded in Court Minutes IOR: B, Reports of the Military Seminary Committee 1809–34 IOR: L/MIL/1/9–16, and minutes of the Political and Military Committee 1834–59 IOR: L/MIL/1/49–74

Lists of Seminary staff appear twice yearly in the *East India register* 1809–61

There are notes on staff members in IOR: L/AG/30/6 & 12 (1817, 1827, 1834–58)

Records of salary payments to the Addiscombe staff 1830–52 are in the series IOR: L/AG/45/2/1. For pensions paid to retired members of staff *see* the series IOR: L/AG/9/4 & L/AG/21/6

PEMBROKE HOUSE AND EALING LUNATIC ASYLUM 1830–1892

For administrative records and records of patients and staff *see* the series IOR: K/2

ROYAL INDIAN ENGINEERING COLLEGE, COOPER'S HILL, 1871–1906

A short history of the Royal Indian Engineering College, Cooper's Hill, John Gordon Patrick Cameron (Cooper's Hill Society, 1960) IOL: T 18632
Calendar of the Royal Indian Engineering College, Cooper's Hill, 1873–1903 IOL: ST 1378
The Cooper's Hill magazine (Cooper's Hill Society, 1943–61) IOL: SV 373

For administrative records and records of staff and students 1871–1907 *see* the series IOR: L/PWD/8

Lists of staff appear in the *Indian Army and Civil Service list* 1872–76, and the *India list* 1877–1906

The *India Office list* 1886–1906 gives short records of service for the President of the College and for most of the Board of Visitors

For records of salary payments *see* the series IOR: L/AG/20/44. IOR: L/AG/45/3 records termination of appointment gratuities, salaries and wages, 1896–1906

India High Commission

Established in 1920

Lists of High Commission staff appear in the *India Office list* 1921–37, and the *India and Burma Office list* 1938–47 – senior staff are included in the brief records of service in these lists

For service details of High Commission staff who had previously served in the India Office *see* the series IOR: L/AG/29/3

There are records of the payment of service pensions to retired High Commission staff 1955–68 in IOR: L/AG/21/1/41–44

The IOR holds the following staff lists:– Apr 1931, Oct 1938, Oct 1939, Apr 1941–Jan 1942, Sep–Dec 1944, Apr 1945–Jun 1946, Aug 1949, Mar 1954, ditto 1956, 1957, 1960, 1964, 1966–68

Covenanted Overseas Civil Servants of The East India Company 1600–1858, The India Office 1858–1947, and The Burma Office 1937–1948

RECORDS OF APPOINTMENT

Pre-1749 records of appointment can be traced in Court Minutes IOR: B, and Correspondence with India IOR: E. For the published abstracts or calendars of the early Court Minutes and Correspondence 1600–79, *see* the introduction to the list of IOR: B in the Catalogue Hall. Despatches from England to Madras 1670–1758, have been published *in extenso,* with indexes

Writers' Petitions 1749–1805, and Committee of College References 1806–56, IOR: J/1/1–90, give details of parentage, education, date of appointment etc. The series is incomplete, especially for the earlier years. It is indexed in *The records of the East India College Haileybury and other institutions,* Anthony Farrington (London, 1976). For the students' careers at the College *see* the whole of the series IOR: J

Details of the recruitment of Indian Civil Service personnel 1855–1946 are to be found in Public and Judicial Home Correspondence 1855–79 IOR: L/P & J/2, Public and Judicial Department Files 1880–1923 IOR: L/P & J/6, and Services & General Department Files and Collections 1924–46 IOR: L/S & G/6–7. They include information on the educational and family background of candidates and lists of marks gained in the ICS examinations. Copies of ICS examination papers and tables of marks appear in the Reports of the Civil Service Commissioners 1858–1938 IOR: V/7/181–250.

Bonds and Agreements, Overseas Servants, 1771–1946 IOR: O/1/1–196 index IOR: Z/O/1/1–5, give dates of appointment and, up to Aug 1875, the names and addresses of two sureties. For Bonds before 1771 *see* Court Minutes IOR: B. From Jul 1876 the index gives dates of birth

COMPILATIONS

Memorials of old Haileybury College, Frederick Charles Danvers & others (London, 1894)
Bengal civil servants 1780–1838, Edward Dodwell & James Samuel Miles (London, 1839)
Register of Bengal civil servants 1790–1842, Henry Thoby Prinsep & Ramchunder Doss (London, 1844)
Record of services of *Madras civilians 1741–1858,* Charles Prinsep (London 1885), contains some details of post-1858 services
Madras civil servants 1780–1839, Edward Dodwell & James Samuel Miles (London, 1839)
Bombay Civil Servants 1780–1839, Edward Dodwell & James Samuel Miles (London, 1839)

For summary careers of Bengal, Madras and Bombay Civilians 1740–1858 by C C Prinsep *see* IOR: 0/6/21–36. Some details of post-1858 services are included

Personal Records *c*1794–*c*1841 IOR: 0/6/1–20, consisting of memoranda prepared at East India House which include records of service and notes on various individuals. Each volume has an index, and there is also a cumulative index IOR: Z/0/6/1–2

Fairly detailed histories of service for Madras civilians appear in the *Madras Asylum Press almanac* from 1862

Histories of Service 1875–1955, IOR: V12, are detailed records of service for ICS personnel and other civil servants of gazetted rank. They are arranged in two separate series, by department and by province, and include dates of appointment, postings, leave etc. As a general rule dates of birth of European members of the ICS are *not* given before *c*1914, and in most of the provincial series this information is only available from *c*1930

Short records of service for serving and retired civilians appear in the *India Office list* from 1886, and from 1929 dates of birth are given for civilians still on active service

OTHER SERVICE RECORDS

The main sources for the early period are Original Correspondence and Correspondence with India

IOR: E, Factory Records IOR: G, and Consultations IOR: P. Despatches to Madras 1670–1758, Madras Consultations 1672–1760, and other early records of the Madras Presidency have been published *in extenso.

Half-yearly establishment lists appear in Bombay Public Proceedings 1712–93 IOR: P, and IOR: 0/6/37 is a typescript copy of these lists 1712–52. There are lists of civil servants 1684–1713 in IOR: D/91–93

IOR: L/F/10, annual lists of Covenanted Civil Servants, covering Bengal 1706–1917, Madras 1702–1801 & 1821–77, and Bombay 1786 & 1797–1877. For a detailed breakdown *see* the list of IOR: L/F in the Catalogue Hall

Civil Lists, IOR: V13, annual or half-yearly establishment lists of the ICS and other civil servants. They are arranged in two separate series, provincial and departmental, and range in date from 1840 to 1957

There is a printed *list of EIC Civil Servants covering all three Presidencies for the years 1771, 1774, 1776, 1780, 1782, 1790, 1795 & 1799. A separate printed *list for 1785 covers the whole of India, there are further lists for the three Presidencies in the *Bengal calendar* for 1792, and *see also* IOR: V/6/1–12

There are separate printed *lists of Bengal Civil Servants for the years 1784–85, 1787, and 1789–90

Lists of Covenanted Civil Servants, with details of postings, appear in the *East India register* 1800–60, the *Indian Army and Civil Service list* 1861–76, the *India list* 1877–1906, the *India Office list* 1907–37, and the *India and Burma Office list* 1938–47

Military Statements IOR: L/MIL/8 include lists of civil establishments for Bengal 1785, 1787, 1789 & 1792–93, Madras 1792–95, 1798–99 & 1801, and Bombay 1792–98

There are lists of eighteenth century establishments in IOR: H/78–79 & 348–60, and *see also* lists of services in IOR: H/764

Home Miscellaneous Series, IOR: H, contains a great deal of correspondence either from or relating to EIC civil servants, especially for the eighteenth century. For Bengal in the eighteenth century much useful information can be obtained from the *Press list of the Bengal Public

Proceedings 1748–1800 published in 21 volumes by the Imperial Records Department, and for Madras see *Vestiges of old Madras 1640–1800*, Henry Davison Love, 4 vols (London, 1913)

Furlough books 1825–1963 (ie records of payments made to civilians while on leave in the UK) in the series IOR: L/AG/20/1 are useful for establishing exact dates of arrival in and departure from the UK

Annuities 1826–1968 (ie service pensions paid to retired ICS personnel in the UK) in the series IOR: L/AG/21/8 (1826–1931) & L/AG/21/9 (1940–1968) sometimes give addresses. Before 1826 *ad hoc* general pensions were occasionally awarded to retired civil servants – *see* the series IOR: L/AG/21/6

FAMILY INFORMATION

Ecclesiastical Returns and civil registrations of births/baptisms, marriages and deaths/burials for all-India 1698–1968, IOR: N. For a more detailed description *see* the booklet 'India Office Records, Ecclesiastical Returns', available free at the IOLR

Returns of births, marriages and deaths for all-India from 1807 in the *East India register* 1808–44

Returns of births, marriages and deaths in the various series of *Directories for Bengal 1814–63, Madras 1811–61, 1876–94 & 1900–04, and Bombay 1806–82, which sometimes give information not contained in the Ecclesiastical Returns, eg a bride's place of origin in the UK – there are gaps in the earlier sequences for Bengal and Bombay

The various published lists of *Indian monumental inscriptions c1600–c1900 cover most of British India and the Princely States. For inscriptions, c1900–c1949, *see* the handlist of the Lloyd Collection, MSS. Eur.F.146

*Marriages at Fort St George, Madras 1680–1815, 'FEP' (Exeter 1907)

*Burials at St Mary's, Madras 1680–1900, Charles Herbert Malden, 4 vols (Madras, 1903–05)

Wills, administrations, probates, inventories and estates
1618–1725 *see* G/40/23
1704–1783 *see* General Proceedings [P] and Mayor's Court Proceedings [P]

1774–1948 *see* L/AG/34/27 (Inventories), L/AG/34/29 (Wills, Administrations, Probates)

The indexes to the above are now available in the Catalogue Hall, with the exception of the index to District Probates, 1866–1910, Z/L/AG/34/12. For Civilians who died in the UK 1788–1972 *see* Probate Books L/AG/33/1–11

Fund records are an important source of family information. They normally provide the following details: dates of birth, marriage and death of subscribers, dates of birth and death of wives (also date of remarriage), dates of birth of children, dates of marriage of daughters, dates of death of unmarried daughters and of sons who died before the age of withdrawing from the fund. The name of a wife's second husband or of a daughter's husband is usually given.

Bengal Civil Fund Established 1804, closed to new subscribers 1885, applied to members of the Bengal Civil Service
IOR: L/AG/23/5/1–2 Family registers of subscribers alive in 1884
IOR: L/AG/23/5/3 List of those receiving pension on 1 Jul 1885 and those subsequently admitted
For payment books 1885–1968, which sometimes give addresses, *see* the series IOR: L/AG/21/25

Madras Civil Fund Established 1787, closed to new subscribers 1882, applied to members of the Madras Civil Service
IOR: L/AG/23/8/1 List of subscribers to 1884, probably complete, entries go back to those who joined the service in 1762, gives dates of marriage and dates of birth of children but no names, contains an index
IOR: L/AG/23/8/2 Register of living subscribers compiled *c*1888, with additions
IOR: L/AG/23/8/3 List of those in receipt of pension on 1 Jul 1886 and those subsequently admitted
For payment books 1886–1968, which sometimes give addresses, *see* the series IOR: L/AG/21/28

Bombay Civil Fund Established 1804, closed to new subscribers 1885, applied to members of the Bombay Civil Service
IOR: L/AG/23/11/16 Family register of living subscribers, compiled *c*1883
IOR: L/AG/23/11/18 List of those in receipt of pension on 1 Apr 1882 and those subsequently admitted

IOR: L/AG/23/11/1–7 Minutes of meetings of subscribers 1830–1882, including lists of subscribers and pensioners
For payment books 1882–1968, which sometimes give addresses, *see* the series IOR: L/AG/21/31

Indian Civil Service Family Pension Fund
Established 1881, applied to all members of the Indian Civil Service. A complete range of family registers 1881–1942 is held by the Crown Agents, who will supply career information on request.
For payment books 1890–1968, which sometimes give addresses, *see* the series IOR: L/AG/21/33

Uncovenanted and other Overseas Civil Servants of The East India Company 1600–1858, The India Office 1858–1947 and The Burma Office 1937–1948

RECORDS OF APPOINTMENT

Appointments of overseas staff who were recruited in the UK before 1858 are recorded in Court Minutes IOR: B. There are some bonds and agreements for such staff, eg engineers, in the Miscellaneous Bonds 1834–65 IOR: 0/1/367–92, index IOR: Z/0/1/11–12. The main series of bonds for covenanted civil servants 1771–1946 IOR: 0/1/1–196, index IOR: Z/0/1/1–5, also includes other categories eg officers of the Educational Service and Forest Service. For certain appointments made in the UK from 1855 to 1946 *see* Contracts and Agreements IOR: L/F/8. Appointments up to 1924 are also recorded in the correspondence and papers of the relevant home departments, eg Public Works Department IOR: L/PWD/2, 6 & 8 for railway staff etc. From 1924 *see* the papers of the Services and General Department, IOR: L/S & G/6. There is also a series of original agreements for miscellaneous appointments in India 1922–49 mainly made through the India High Commission, IOR: 0/1/393–411.

L/F/8/1–20 UK appointments to Indian Public Works Dept, Government Railways, Telegraph Dept etc. 1854–1946. Indexes, Z/L/F/8/1–2, also card index in progress

Indian Police Prior to 1893 appointments to all senior grades (ie Assistant District Superintendent and above) were made locally in India, and a record of the appointment may appear in the Proceedings [P] of the relevant province. From 1893 most new entrants to the top échelon were appointed by examination or selection in the UK. For the appointment papers, 1893–1923, *see* L/PJ/6; 1924–1940, L/SG/6. The agreements made on appointment between probationers and the Secretary of State, 1893–1937, are to be found in 0/1/164–95, indexes Z/0/1/3–4

RECORDS OF SERVICE

For the early period information on subordinate civil staff can be obtained from Factory Records

IOR: G, and Proceedings IOR: P. Proceedings and other records relating to Madras 1670–1760 have been published *in extenso*. IOR: 0/5/29 records Madras Uncovenanted Civil Servants 1757–77

Some subordinate civil staff are noted in eighteenth century establishment lists in IOR: H/78–79, 238 & 348–360

Some subordinate staff of the civil (to 1801 only) and military departments of all three Presidencies are recorded in the Military Statements 1785–1859, IOR: L/MIL/8

For references to assistants in Bengal public offices in the second half of the eighteenth century see *also* the *Press list of Bengal Public Proceedings 1748–1800,* published in 21 volumes by the Imperial Records Department

There are annual or twice-yearly lists of departmental staff in the *East India register 1800–60,* *Indian Army and Civil Service list 1861–76,* *India list 1877–1906,* *India Office list 1907–37* and *India and Burma Office list 1938–47* – short records of service for civil servants of gazetted rank appear from 1886

Some subordinate civil staff in Bengal are recorded in the *Bengal Calendar* for 1790 and 1792. There are lists of assistants in public offices in the *Bengal directory* for 1814 and from 1820, and in the *Bombay directory* 1829–32 and from 1842. Regular lists of Madras uncovenanted staff do not appear in the *Madras Almanac* before 1860 but there are lists 1818–20 in IOR: 0/5/30

IOR: L/F/10, annual lists of uncovenanted civil servants arranged by province or department, covering 1818–1900 and 1922–28 – they vary considerably in the amount of information provided, which can include age, whether or not born in India, whether European or Eurasian, whether married, date of entering Government service and details of salary

Civil Lists 1840–1957, IOR: V13, annual or twice yearly published lists of civil establishments arranged by province or department – details on the posts of all grades from the ICS down to quite low-level staff

Histories of Service 1875–1955, IOR: V12, detailed records of service for all Government staff of gazetted rank, arranged by province or department, giving details of appointment, postings, dates of leave, and in some cases domicile. Dates of birth are normally given for all non-ICS personnel. Additional information on the Indian Police can be found in IOR: MSS Eur F141

Furlough books 1825–1963 (ie records of payments made to government servants on leave in the UK) in the series IOR: L/AG/20/1 include military and medical officers in civil employment

Service pensions paid to retired uncovenanted servants in the UK before Oct 1860 are recorded in the General Pensions series IOR: L/AG/9/4, and for service pensions 1860–1968 *see* the series IOR: L/AG/21/9, which sometimes gives addresses

FAMILY INFORMATION

See the general sources listed on pp 11–12

Deaths in the Uncovenanted Service 1870–1949, IOR: L/AG/34/14A/1–17. At first applied only to members of the Uncovenanted Service but later extended to cover most other Government officers and European pensioners. Information generally recorded includes date and place of death, age, place of birth and details of surviving relatives and there is a card index to the series.

For military and medical officers seconded to civil employment *see* the notes on military funds on pp 17, 18

Bengal and Madras Service Family Pension Fund Established 1904, open to all men in the service of the Imperial and Provincial Governments in India *except* the ICS, Army and Navy officers, Bombay servants not liable for transfer, and subscribers to the Bengal or Bombay Uncovenanted Service Family Pension Funds. For payment books 1920–1967 *see* IOR: L/AG/21/9/151–57, and for administrative books, IOR: L/AG/23/15

Superior Services Family Pension Fund Established 1928, applied to European members of the superior services other than the ICS, optional for those in service in 1928, compulsory for those who

joined subsequently. A complete range of family registers 1928–43 is held by the Crown Agents who will supply career information on request. For payment books 1928–68, which sometimes give addresses, *see* the series IOR: L/AG/21/33 & 34

European Officers of The East India Company's Armies 1708–1861, and The Indian Army 1861–1947

RECORDS OF APPOINTMENT

For early appointments to the EIC Armies (sometimes made locally in India) *see* Court Minutes IOR: B, Committee of Correspondence records IOR: D, Correspondence with India IOR: E, Factory Records IOR: G, and Proceedings IOR: P. Correspondence and proceedings relating to the Madras Presidency 1670–1760 have been published *in extenso* by the Madras Government, and for indexes to Despatches to Bengal, Madras and Bombay, 1753–1858, *see* IOR: Z/E/4/1–72

The main series recording the appointment of officers to the EIC armies is the Cadet Papers 1789–1860, IOR: L/MIL/9/107–253. From about 1795 they include details of birth/baptism and education. There is a complementary series of Cadet Registers 1775–1860, IOR: L/MIL/9/255–269 which provides summary details, eg date of appointment, list of rank. A cumulative index to both the Cadet Papers and the early Cadet Registers is available in the Catalogue Hall

Records of the education of cadets at the Royal Military Academy Woolwich 1798–1808, Addiscombe Military Seminary 1809–61, and the Royal Engineers' Institution Chatham 1815–62, IOR: L/MIL/1/9–80 & L/MIL/9/333–57. Attendance at Addiscombe Military Seminary was compulsory for Artillery and Engineer cadets, optional for Cavalry and Infantry cadets

Appointment papers for Queen's/King's India Cadetships at Sandhurst 1858–1930, cadets commissioned onto the Indian Army Unattached List from Sandhurst 1901–40, and cadets trained at Wellington and Quetta in India 1915–19, *see* IOR: L/MIL/9/292–332. All these papers provide information on a cadet's family background. It should be noted however that apart from Queen's India Cadets there are no appointment papers for officers commissioned into the Indian Army 1863–1900

Application papers of officers appointed to temporary commissions in the Indian Army 1919–21, *see* IOR: L/MIL/9/435–551, index IOR: Z/L/MIL/9/6, which is also available in the Catalogue Hall

Appointments to the Indian Army Reserve of Officers from the British Army 1917–18, *see* IOR: L/MIL/9/552–623, index IOR: Z/L/MIL/9/7, which is also available in the Catalogue Hall

RECORDS OF SERVICE – COMPILATIONS

The East India military calendar, containing the services of general and field officers of the Indian Army, John Philippart, 3 vols (London, 1823–26)

Alphabetical list of the officers of the Indian Army . . . 1760–1834, with corrections to 1837, Edward Dodwell & James Samuel Miles (London, 1838)

Bengal Army Officers 1834–62, IOR: 0/6/38–39, manuscript summaries of careers in continuation of Dodwell & Miles

List of officers of the Bengal Army 1758–1834, Vernon Charles Paget Hodson, 4 vols (London, 1927–28 & 1946–47), contains detailed biographical notes on each officer

'Ubique': war services of all the officers of HM Bengal Army Thomas Carnegy Anderson (Calcutta, 1863) confined to officers still serving in 1863, includes notes on officers who did not see active service

List of officers who have served in the Bengal Artillery 1745–1860, Francis William Stubbs (Bath, 1892) gives dates of promotion, retirement and death

Biographical notices of officers of the Royal Bengal Engineers, Edward Talbot Thackeray (London, 1900), contains biographies of distinguished officers of the EIC (later Royal) Bengal Engineers 1756–1890

List of officers who have served in the Madras Artillery 1748–1861, John Henry Leslie (Leicester,

1900), gives dates of promotion, retirement and death

*List of officers who have served in the Bombay Artillery 1749–1861, Frederick William Mackenzie Spring (London, 1902), gives service details as well as dates of promotion, retirement and death

Part II of *A list of inscriptions on Christian tombs or monuments in the Punjab (including Delhi), North-West Frontier Province, Kashmir and Afghanistan, Miles Irving (Lahore, 1910), contains detailed biographical notices of all officers whose monumental inscriptions (c1800–c1905) are noted in Part I

The historical records of the Survey of India, Reginald Henry Phillimore, 5 vols (Dehra Dun, 1945–68), contains appendices of biographical notes on EIC officers who served in the Survey 1767–1861

Personal records, c1794–c1841, IOR: O/6/1–20, each volume indexed, cumulative index IOR: Z/0/6/1–2, a series of memoranda prepared at East India House including service records and notes on EIC officers

Quite detailed statements of service often accompany the formal requests to retire on pension, which appear in Auditor's References, 1799–1835, D/153–252, indexes, Z/D/28–32. These are especially useful for officers who retired before 1830, most of whom are excluded from the Service Army Lists

Bengal, Madras and Bombay Service Army Lists. Detailed service records in two sections – cumulative, followed by annual additions. They do not include officers retired or dead before 1830
Bengal 1770–1858, IOR: L/MIL/10/20–69, index IOR: Z/L/MIL/10/1 cumulative to 1843, annual additions to 1858
Madras 1771–1859, IOR: L/MIL/11/38–69, index IOR: Z/L/MIL/11/1, cumulative to 1846, annual additions to 1859
Bombay 1770–1859, IOR: L/MIL/12/67–84, index IOR: Z/L/MIL/12/1, cumulative to 1852, annual additions to 1859

Bengal, Madras and Bombay Services. Detailed service records forwarded when the officer concerned took furlough in Europe.
Bengal 1860–93, IOR: L/MIL/10/75–102, index IOR: Z/L/MIL/10/2

Madras 1860–92, IOR: L/MIL/11/73–92, index IOR: Z/L/MIL/11/2
Bombay 1860–92, IOR: L/MIL/12/88–101, index IOR: Z/L/MIL/12/2

Indian Army Service Statements 1892–1916, IOR: L/MIL/14/1–49, index IOR: Z/L/MIL/14/1–2, brief records of service, mainly details of previous leave, for officers taking furlough in Europe

Statements of war services occur intermittently in Bengal, Madras and Bombay Army lists, IOR: L/MIL/17/2–4, from about 1855. They are continued in the *Indian Army list Oct 1889–Jul 1919 and in *Indian Army list supplements Jan 1902–Jan 1942

Indian Army Records of Service c1900–50, IOR: L/MIL/14/237 et seq, mainly post-1930 personal files, they include regular officers of the Indian Army, Second World War Emergency Commissioned Officers, and certain Warrant and Honorary Officers. The files are not normally available for public use but career information may be supplied upon request

For regular officers seconded to civil employment see also pp 13–14

OTHER SERVICE RECORDS

Officers are occasionally recorded in Muster Rolls:
Bengal Army 1716–1861, IOR: L/MIL/10/130–85
Madras Army 1762 & 1765, IOR: L/MIL/11/109
Bombay Army 1708–1865, IOR: L/MIL/12/117–97

There are manuscript and published Army Lists, as follows:
Bengal Army 1781–1849, IOR: L/MIL/10/1–19
published Bengal Army list 1819–89, IOR: L/MIL/17/2
Madras Army 1759–1846, IOR: L/MIL/11/1–37
published *Madras Army list for 1804
published Madras Army list 1810–95, IOR: L/MIL/17/3
Bombay Army 1759–1855, IOR: L/MIL/12/1–17
published Bombay Army list 1823–95, IOR: L/MIL/17/4
published *Indian Army list 1889–1947

Lists of officers of the Bengal, Madras and Bombay Armies, arranged by regiment, appear in the Military Statements 1785–1859, IOR: L/MIL/8

The *Bengal calendar* for 1792 lists officers of the Bengal, Madras and Bombay Armies, and lists of the Bengal Military Establishment appear in the *Civil and military list* for 1784–85 and 1787, and in the *Bengal calendar* for 1789–90

Annual or half-yearly lists of officers appear in the *East India register* 1800–60, the *Indian Army and Civil Service list* 1861–76, and the *India list* 1877–95

The Home Miscellaneous Series, IOR: H, contains lists of eighteenth century officers and also a great deal of correspondence relating to individual officers

There are casualty returns for Bengal Army officers 1786–1895, IOR: L/MIL/10/103–07; Madras Army officers 1800–95, IOR: L/MIL/11/93–98; Bombay Army officers 1842–95, IOR: L/MIL/12/102–05; and Indian Army officers 1895–1948, IOR: L/MIL/14/137–43. Casualties are also noted in the published Army Lists to 1946 and in the *East India register* etc to 1895

For furlough books 1795–1947, ie records of payments made to officers while on leave in the UK, *see* the series IOR: L/AG/20/6
Officers in civil employment are covered in the series IOR: L/AG/20/1

For records of pensions paid to retired officers in the UK before 1825 *see* the series General Pensions IOR: L/AG/21/6, the records of the Lord Clive Fund IOR: L/AG/23/2, and Colonels' Allowances below. For service pensions 1825–1968 *see* the series IOR: L/AG/21/11, which sometimes gives addresses. Officers admitted to pension in India 1898–1913, *see* L/AG/26/14/1, *ditto*, widows and children, L/AG/26/15/1. For payment books of pensions in the Dominions/Colonies, 1860–1970, *see* the series L/AG/21/44, and for Canada/USA 1952–69, *see* the series L/AG/21/43

Some officers commissioned before 1881 and who attained the rank of Lieutenant-Colonel or above were never technically retired but were placed on the Unemployed List and received a Colonel's Allowance as well as unemployment pay. The series IOR: L/AG/21/12 records the payment of Colonels' Allowances 1803–1948 (originally called Off-Reckonings), sometimes giving addresses – the draft guide to IOR: L/AG, available in the Catalogue Hall, contains an historical explanation of the system

Release leave accounts for Second World War Emergency Commissioned Officers 1945–47, divided into UK releases IOR: L/AG/20/29/1–39, and Colonial releases IOR: L/AG/20/31/1–2, are useful for establishing the exact date when an EC officer relinquished his commission. They also record payment of war gratuities

FAMILY INFORMATION

See the general sources listed on pp 11–12

Military Wills etc. Officers and other ranks of the EIC/Indian Army appear in the general series of Wills and Inventories etc [L/AG/34/29 and 27] but there is also a separate military series, viz:– 1) Treasury Deposits 1792–1927, L/AG/34/33, indexed at Z/L/AG/34/17–21, 2) Military Estate Papers, 1850–1937, L/AG/34/40, and 3) Soldiers' Wills, 1820–1881, L/AG/34/30. The most useful of these are the Military Estate Papers, which include, as well as estate accounts, wills, inventories and lists of wives and children. They are not indexed, properly speaking, but can be approached via the indexes to Treasury Deposits

Lord Clive Fund Also described as Military (late Lord Clive) Fund, established 1770, provided benefits for retired officers and their widows, but not children. For lists of pensioners, payment books, etc, *see* the series IOR: L/AG/21/10 & L/AG/23/2. A modern index is available

Bengal Military Fund Established 1824, closed to new subscribers 1862, compulsory for combatant ranks from Aug 1826, related to widows only IOR: LA/G/23/6/1 Register of subscribers 1824–62, records dates of birth, marriage and death of subscriber and wife, names of wives not given but these may usually be found in pay books, subscription ledgers, etc
IOR: L/AG/23/6/2 List of widows receiving pension c1860–65
IOR: L/AG/23/6/3–6 Registers of pensioners from 1866 to the end of the fund
IOR: L/AG/23/6/8–11 Ledgers of subscriptions from 1867, containing details of marriage, index IOR: L/AG/23/6/12
For payment books 1836–1968, which sometimes give addresses, *see* the series IOR: L/AG/1/14 & L/AG/21/26

Bengal Military Orphan Society Established 1783, closed to new subscribers 1861, subscriptions compulsory from Apr 1807, related to children (both legitimate and illegitimate)

IOR: L/AG/23/7/7 Two lists of orphans c1820

IOR: L/AG/23/7/8 List of orphans in England 1828

IOR: L/AG/23/7/9 List of orphans 1856–66

IOR: L/AG/23/7/10–13 Registers of orphans from 1866 to the end of the fund

IOR: L/AG/23/7/15–19 Registers of subscriptions with details of subscribers' children from 1856 to the end of the fund, index IOR: L/AG/23/6/12

IOR: L/AG/23/7/20 Returns of births, marriages and deaths of children, plus list of orphans in India, 1877–1907

For payment books 1866–1968, which sometimes give addresses, *see* the series IOR: L/AG/21/27

Madras Military Fund Established 1808, closed to new subscribers 1862

IOR: L/AG/23/10/1–2 Complete rolls of subscribers and of their wives and children

IOR: L/AG/23/10/7–10 Registers of pensioners from 1866 to the end of the fund

For payment books 1832–1968, which sometimes give addresses, *see* the series IOR: L/AG/1/14 & L/AG/21/30

Bombay Military Fund Established 1816, closed to new subscribers 1862

IOR: L/AG/23/12/1–4 Family registers of subscribers who had left India by the 1860s. Each volume is indexed and there is a cumulative index, IOR: L/AG/23/12/5

IOR: L/AG/23/12/6 Lists of subscribers, 1858, 1866 & 1875

IOR: L/AG/23/12/10–13 Registers of pensioners from 1866 to the end of the fund

For payment books 1851–1968, which sometimes give addresses, see the series IOR: L/AG/1/14 & L/AG/21/32

Indian Military Service Family Pension Fund Established 1873, closed to new subscribers 1914

IOR: L/AG/23/16/4–9 Family register of all who joined between 1873 and Mar 1893, index IOR: L/AG/23/16/10

IOR: L/AG/23/16/31–43 Copies of the family registers 1893–1914

For payment books 1873–1968, which sometimes give addresses, *see* the series IOR: L/AG/21/35

Indian Military Widows' and Orphans' Fund Established 1915, last subscriber joined 1943

A complete range of family registers 1915–43 is held by the Crown Agents, who will supply career information on request

For payment books 1919–68, which sometimes give addresses, *see* the series IOR: L/AG/21/36

Family information is also recorded in personal records of service, IOR: L/MIL/14, which are particularly useful for Emergency Commissioned Officers (who did not contribute to the Military Funds) especially as during the Second World War the system of Ecclesiastical Returns began to break down

Departmental and Warrant Officers
of The East India Company's Armies 1708–1861,
and the Indian Army 1861–1947

Warrant officers in the Company's armies held the ranks of Sub-Conductor and Conductor, serving mainly in the Ordnance, Commissariat and Public Works Departments. They were recruited from the Town Major's List (called Effective Supernumeraries in Madras) which in turn was largely recruited from the NCOs of the Company's European regiments (see p 21) although occasionally NCOs of British regiments stationed in India were appointed to it.

In 1859 the Town Major's List became the Unattached List, and when the Company's European regiments were amalgamated with the British Army in 1860 new recruits to the Unattached List were appointed solely from NCOs of British regiments stationed in India.

Conductors were eligible for promotion to Departmental Officer, ie Deputy Assistant Commissary, Assistant Commissary etc, and these grades were eventually given complementary honorary officer ranks ranging from Honorary Lieutenant to Honorary Major.

RECORDS OF SERVICE

There are lists of Bengal Army Conductors of Ordnance and Deputy Commissaries in the *India (Bengal) calendar* 1789 and the *Bengal calendar* for 1790 and 1792

Conductors and departmental officers in all three Presidencies are recorded in the *East India register* 1800–60, *Indian Army and Civil Service list* 1861–76, and *India list* 1877–95, which also gives Sub-Conductors

Some warrant and departmental officers appear in Military Statements 1785–1859, IOR: L/MIL/8

Army Lists and Muster Rolls
Bengal Departmental officers, Conductors and Sub-Conductors are given in the published *Bengal Army list* from 1819, IOR: L/MIL/17/2
Madras Departmental officers and Conductors are given in the published *Madras Army list* for 1804

and from 1810 onwards, IOR: L/MIL/17/3. Sub-Conductors, who first appear in the published list in 1827, are noted in the Madras Muster Rolls 1820–1830, IOR: L/MIL/11/128–37

Bombay Departmental officers, Conductors and Sub-Conductors appear in the published *Bombay Army list* from 1828, IOR: L/MIL/17/4, and there are lists of Conductors and Sub-Conductors in Bombay Muster Rolls 1812–34, IOR: L/MIL/12/140–58

India All departmental and warrant officers are recorded in the *Indian Army list* 1889–1947

Departmental and warrant officers who served in the Public Works Department are also recorded in the PWD Civil Lists 1861–1940, IOR: V13. Dates of birth appear from Jun 1882

Directories Departmental officers and Conductors appear in the *Bengal directory* from 1815, and Sub-Conductors from 1820. There is a list of departmental officers and Conductors in the *Madras almanac* 1800 and lists of all Madras departmental and warrant officers appear in the *Asylum Press almanac* from 1862. The *Bombay directory* records departmental officers and Conductors from 1823, Sub-Conductors from 1829.

By a Royal Warrant of 1882 British Army Sergeant-Majors or Quarter-Master Sergeants were appointed to non-departmental posts in the Indian Army. These non-departmental warrant officers are shown in the published *Bengal, Madras* and *Bombay Army lists* from 1882, IOR: L/MIL/17/2–4, and in the *Indian Army list* from Oct 1889. They also appear in the *India list* 1883–95; the Bengal Unattached Lists 1895–1907, IOR: L/MIL/10/233–52; Bombay Unattached Lists 1902–07, IOR: L/MIL/12/275–80; Indian Army Unattached Lists 1908–39, IOR: L/MIL/14/144–74

Records of service of a few departmental and warrant officers who took leave to Europe appear in the series Bengal Services 1860–92, IOR:

L/MIL/10/75–102, index IOR: Z/L/MIL/10/2; Madras Services 1860–92, IOR: L/MIL/11/73–92, index Z/L/MIL/11/2; Bombay Services 1860–92, IOR: L/MIL/12/88-101, index IOR: Z/L/MIL/12/2

Quite detailed records of previous service for departmental and warrant officers who took leave to Europe 1892–1916 appear in the series Indian Army Service Statements, IOR: L/MIL/14/1–49, index IOR: Z/L/MIL/14/1–2

Indian Army Records of Service (Personal Files) *c*1900–1950, IOR: L/MIL/14/237 *et seq*, include departmental and warrant officers. They generally cover the period after 1920 but some service records of the Indian Miscellaneous List include men who joined as early as 1870. These files are not normally available to the public but information from them can be supplied upon request

There are records of war services of departmental and warrant officers in the published Army Lists: Bengal 1884–89, IOR: L/MIL/17/2; Madras 1861–95, IOR: L/MIL/17/3; Bombay 1868–83, IOR: L/MIL/17/4. They are continued in the *Indian Army list* Oct 1889–Jul 1919 and in the *Indian Army list supplements* Jan 1902–Jan 1942. From 1899 services of departmental officers (but not warrant officers) are included in the sections covering regular officers of the Indian Army

For furlough books 1825–1947, ie records of payments made to departmental and warrant officers on leave in the UK, *see* the series IOR: L/AG/20/9 (1825–1939) & L/AG/20/6 (1939–47)

For records of service pensions paid to retired departmental and warrant officers in the UK 1825–1968, *see* the series IOR: L/AG/21/13 (1825–1958) & L/AG/21/11 (1958–68). Addresses are sometimes given
D. and W. Officers admitted to pension in India, 1883–1914, *see* L/AG/26/14/2–4, *ditto* wives and children 1883–1908, L/AG/26/15/2–4. Payments of pensions in Colonies/Dominions, 1860–1970 *see* the series L/AG/21/43 and 44

FAMILY INFORMATION

See the general sources listed on pp 11–12

Lord Clive Fund, set up in 1770, was the only official fund applicable to departmental and warrant officers. It provided benefits for retired officers, NCOs, private soldiers, and their widows, but not children. For lists of pensioners, payment books etc *see* the series IOR: L/AG/21/10 & L/AG/23/2

Royal Warrant pensions were paid, from 1886, to widows and orphans of departmental and warrant officers who joined the service after 1881. Records of payments in the UK appear in the Indian Military Service Family Pensions Fund payment books, IOR: L/AG/21/35

The note on Military Wills etc on p 17 above applies also to Departmental and Warrant Officers

See also Indian Army Records of Service above

European NCOs and Privates
of The East India Company's Armies 1708–1861
and the Indian Army 1861–1947

Before 1801, when Registers of Recruits begin, the main source of information on the recruitment of European private soldiers for the EIC European Artillery and Infantry Regiments are the Embarkation Lists 1753–1861, IOR: L/MIL/9/85–106. The following volumes in particular supply details of place of origin before 1801: IOR: L/MIL/9/85 (1753–63), L/MIL/9/89–90 (1774–84), L/MIL/9/96 (1792–97) and L/MIL/9/103–04 (1778–86). Embarkation Lists also record the names of the few wives and children who accompanied recruits to India. The Registers of European Soldiers 1788–1860 record place of origin but they do not include soldiers who died before 1831, and the Muster Rolls also give place of origin

Registers of Recruits There are Depot Registers (arranged alphabetically) of Infantry recruits 1801–60, IOR: L/MIL/9/37–46, Artillery recruits 1811–60, IOR: L/MIL/9/29–34, and Cavalry recruits 1857–60, IOR: L/MIL/9/35–36. There is also a series of registers arranged chronologically and by recruiting district 1817–60, IOR: L/MIL/9/1–28. Both series give details of a recruit's place of birth (town and/or parish), age, and former employment, together with a physical description

Unattached Lists In 1860 the EIC European regiments were amalgamated with the British Army and there was then no direct recruitment of European private soldiers to the Indian Army. The only European other ranks were NCOs on the Unattached List, who held various departmental and non-departmental appointments. Most of the NCOs on the old EIC Town Majors' Lists (styled Effective Supernumeraries in Madras) remained on the Unattached List, but new appointments from 1859 were made from NCOs of British Army regiments stationed in India

There are annual Unattached Lists as follows: Bengal Army 1859–1907, IOR: L/MIL/10/201–52; Madras Army 1863–1907, IOR: L/MIL/11/186–231;

Bombay Army 1860–1907, IOR: L/MIL/12/209–280; Indian Army 1908–44, IOR: L/MIL/14/144–75. They give details of recruitment (whether to the EIC Armies or the British Army) and present posting. Before 1906 they generally give details of age and place of birth

NCOs on the Unattached List were eligible for promotion to Sub-Conductor (warrant officer) and above and might eventually attain honorary officer rank (*see* p 19)

Muster Rolls and Casualty Returns There are Muster Rolls and Casualty Returns for NCOs and privates of the Bengal Army 1716–1861, IOR: L/MIL/10/130–85; Madras Army 1762–1861, IOR: L/MIL/11/109–69; Bombay army 1708–1865; IOR: L/MIL/12/117–97. Beginning as brief nominal rolls, they give more details from 1765 (Madras) and 1769 (Bengal and Bombay), recording the battalion or troop to which each soldier was attached. They also include casualty lists and lists of invalids, pensioners and NCOs on the Town Majors' Lists/Effective Supernumeraries. Bengal Muster Rolls give a soldier's town/parish of origin from Oct 1816, and Madras Muster Rolls from Jan 1823. Bombay Muster Rolls give a soldier's county of origin from 1802

Registers of East India Company European Soldiers Bengal 1788–1860, IOR: L/MIL/10/122–29; Madras 1786–1860, IOR: L/MIL/11/101–08; Bombay 1795–1862, IOR: L/MIL/12/109–16. They give personal details of enlisted men, including place of origin, in a roughly alphabetical order by year of arrival, but they do not, however, include soldiers who died before 1831

Discharge papers of soldiers who took the option of unpensioned discharge when the EIC's European troops were amalgamated with the British Army 1859–61: Bengal Army IOR:

L/MIL/10/303–17; Madras Army IOR: L/MIL/11/278–81; Bombay Army IOR: L/MIL/12/282–86. The records of service in the discharge papers are more detailed than those in the general registers (*see* above), and they include details of active service

The services of European NCOs in the Indian Army after 1859 can be traced year by year through the Unattached Lists (*see* above), and there are records of service for those who were promoted to warrant officer (*see* p 19). For services of Sergeants in the Public Works Department *see* p 19

Records of service pensions paid to retired EIC/Indian Army NCOs and privates in India from 1861 appear in Bengal, Madras, Bombay and Indian Unattached Lists 1861–1921 (*see* above). For service pensions paid in India before 1861 *see* Muster Rolls above, and for pensioners in the UK *see* note on Lord Clive Fund below

There are separate casualty returns for NCOs and privates (both active and retired): Bengal Army 1800–1907, IOR: L/MIL/10/186–92, 253–300, Madras Army 1853–1907, IOR: L/MIL/11/232–76, Bombay Army 1855–1907, IOR: L/MIL/12/198–265

FAMILY INFORMATION

See the general sources listed on pp 11–12

Wills, administrations, probates, inventories and estates, 1618–1950, in the series IOR: L/AG/34. Information on NCOs and privates is more likely to be found in the military section – *see* Soldiers' Wills, Treasury Deposits, and Military Estate Papers. The Estate Papers 1850–1937, IOR: L/AG/34/40, are especially useful. They record some extremely small estates of NCOs and privates and often give names of widows and children. The index to Treasury Deposits also serves as a *rough* index to Estate Papers

The only official fund for NCOs and privates was the Lord Clive Fund, set up in 1770. It provided benefits for retired NCOs, privates, and their widows, but not children. For lists of pensioners, payment books etc, *see* the series IOR: L/AG/23/2 & L/AG/21/10: Admissions to Lord Clive pensions in UK 1830–1882 *see* L/AG/23/2/65–66 (includes women pensioners from 1861). Deaths of Lord Clive pensioners in UK 1820–1882 *see* L/AG/23/2/67–69. Payments of Lord Clive pensions in UK 1829–1881 *see* L/AG/35/50–54. Payments of Lord Clive pensions in UK 1882–1937 *see* L/AG/21/45/1–8.

Medical and Veterinary Officers
of the East India Company's Armies 1708–1861,
and The Indian Army 1861–1947

Early appointments of EIC army surgeons must be sought in Court Minutes IOR: B, Committee of Correspondence records IOR: D, General Correspondence IOR: E, Factory Records IOR: G, and Proceedings IOR: P. Correspondence and proceedings relating to the Madras Presidency 1670–1760 have been published *in extenso, with indexes, by the Madras Government, and there are indexes to Despatches to Bengal, Madras and Bombay 1753–1858, IOR: Z/E/4/1–72

The main series of appointment records for medical officers are the Assistant-Surgeons' and Surgeons' Papers 1804–1914, IOR: L/MIL/9/358–408 & 413–27, index IOR: Z/L/MIL/9/5, which is also available in the Catalogue Hall. They include details of birth/baptism and education. There are complementary annual lists of Assistant Surgeons 1787–1814, IOR: L/MIL/9/409–10, and 1815–60, IOR: L/MIL/9/260–69

Veterinary Surgeons were first appointed to the EIC Armies in 1826. There is a series of Veterinary Surgeons' Papers 1826–59, IOR: L/MIL/9/433, consisting of petitions, certificates of age, testimonials and related correspondence

Surgeons are recorded in the series of bonds for EIC officials 1771–1827, IOR: O/1/1–79, index IOR: Z/0/1/1. These give the names and addresses of two sureties

RECORDS OF SERVICE – COMPILATIONS

* Alphabetical list of Indian medical officers 1764–1838, Edward Dodwell & James Samuel Miles (London, 1839) records dates of appointment, promotions, retirement or death

* Roll of the Indian Medical Service 1615–1930, Dirom Grey Crawford (London, 1930), records educational qualifications, dates of birth, appointment and promotions, and details of war services

* History of the Indian Medical Service, Dirom Grey Crawford, 2 vols (London, 1914), includes biographical details of distinguished members of the IMS

Part II of * A list of inscriptions on Christian tombs or monuments in the Punjab (including Delhi), North-West Frontier Province, Kashmir and Afghanistan, Miles Irving (Lahore, 1910) contains biographical notices of all surgeons whose monumental inscriptions are given in Part I

Personal Records c1794–c1841, IOR: O/6/1–20. A series of memoranda prepared at East India House, including records of service and notes on army surgeons. Each volume has an index and there is also a cumulative index, IOR: Z/O/6/1–2

Service Army Lists (Medical)
Detailed records of service of Surgeons and Assistant-Surgeons, arranged alphabetically:
Bengal c1765–1858, IOR: L/MIL/10/70–74. The first three volumes cover those dead or in retirement c1855, the last two those still serving, with additions to 1858
Madras c1760–1858, IOR: L/MIL/11/70–72
Bombay 1763–1858, IOR: L/MIL/12/85–87. The first volume covers serving officers 1788–1858, and the other two cover deceased or retired officers 1763–1858

Bengal, Madras and Bombay Services contain detailed records of service forwarded when an IMS officer took furlough in Europe:
Bengal Services 1860–93, IOR: L/MIL/10/75–102, index IOR: Z/L/MIL/10/2
Madras Services 1860–92, IOR: L/MIL/11/73–92, index IOR: Z/L/MIL/11/2
Bombay Services 1860–92, IOR: L/MIL/12/88–101, index IOR: Z/L/MIL/12/2

Indian Army Service Statements 1892–1916, IOR: L/MIL/14/1–49, index IOR: Z/L/MIL/14/1–2, contain brief records of service, mainly details of previous leave, for IMS officers taking furlough to Europe

Statements of war services occur intermittently in

published *Bengal, Madras* and *Bombay Army lists,* IOR: L/MIL/17/2–4, from about 1855 onwards. They are continued in the *Indian Army list* from Oct 1889 to Jul 1919 (in the Jan and Jul issues only from Jul 1904) and in *Indian Army list supplements* from Jan 1902 to Jan 1942

Indian Army Records of Service (Personal Files) *c*1900–1950, IOR: L/MIL/14/237 *et seq*, include officers of the Indian Medical Service. The majority date from after 1930, particularly the Second World War period. These files are not normally available for public use but career information can be supplied upon request

Records of service for IMS officers who were Civil Surgeons appear in the *India Office* list from 1886 and in Histories of Service (*see* p 14)

OTHER SERVICE RECORDS

For the early period *see* Factory Records IOR: G, and Proceedings IOR: P. Correspondence and Proceedings relating to Madras 1670–1760 have been published *in extenso*, with indexes, by the Madras Government and *see also Vestiges of old Madras 1640–1700*, Henry Davison Love, 4 vols (London, 1913). Surgeons are recorded in the half-yearly lists of establishments in Bombay Public Proceedings 1712–93, IOR: P, and IOR: 0/6/37 is a typescript copy of these lists 1712–52

There are lists of surgeons in India in the Home Miscellaneous Series, IOR: H/78 (1749, 1754 & 1700), H/90 (1781 & 1789) & H/358–61 (*c*1776–83)

Lists of surgeons at each Presidency appear in the *Bengal calendar* 1792 and there are separate *lists of Bengal surgeons for 1784–85, 1787, 1789 & 1790

Annual or half-yearly lists of the Indian medical establishment appear in the *East India register* 1800–60, the *Indian Army and Civil Service list* 1861–76, and the *India List* 1877–95

IMS officers are also listed in the *Bengal, Madras* and *Bombay Army Lists,* IOR: L/MIL/17/2–4, and in the *Indian Army List* 1889–1947

IMS officers holding civil posts are listed in the *India list* 1896–1906, the *India Office list* 1907–37, and the *India and Burma Office list* 1938–47

Furlough Books 1795–1893 *see* L/AG/20/10; 1893–1947 *see* L/AG/20/6. For medical officers in civil employment *see* L/AG/20/1

Pension Books UK Service Pensions, 1825–1956 *see* L/AG/21/15; 1956–1968 *see* L/AG/21/11

Medical Officers admitted to pension in India, 1898–1913, *see* L/AG/26/14/1, *ditto,* wives and children, L/AG/26/15/1. Payments of pensions in the Colonies/Dominions, 1860–1970, *see* the series L/AG/21/43 and 44

FAMILY INFORMATION

See the general sources listed on pp 11–12

Wills, administrations, inventories and estates 1618–1948, IOR: L/AG/34 – both the general and military sections should be consulted

Lord Clive Fund, established 1770 *see* p 17

Bengal Military Fund, established 1824 *see* p 17

Bengal Military Orphan Society, established 1783 *see* p 17

Madras Military Fund, established 1808, *optional* for Madras medical officers up to 1847 *see* p 18

Madras Medical Fund, established 1807, *compulsory* for Madras medical officers from 1823, wound-up in 1870
IOR: L/AG/23/9/3 Family register of married subscribers 1872
IOR: L/AG/23/9/1–2 Register of pensioners from 1870 to the end of the fund
For payment books 1849–1965, which sometimes give addresses, *see* the series IOR: L/AG/21/29

Bombay Military Fund, established 1816 *see* p 18

Indian Military Service Family Pension Fund, established 1873 *see* p 18

Indian Military Widows' and Orphans' Fund, established 1915 *see* p 18

Note Veterinary officers contributed to the Military Funds

Indian Subordinate Medical Service

A Military Subordinate Medical Department was set up in Bengal and Madras in 1812 and a little later in Bombay. Recruits were mainly locally-born of European or Eurasian parentage, but occasionally came from the ranks of the EIC European regiments or British Army regiments stationed in India. The rank of Assistant-Surgeon, which was abolished in the Indian Medical Service in 1873, was introduced into the Military Subordinate Medical Department in 1894, when it replaced the title of Apothecary

RECORDS OF SERVICE

Members of the Subordinate Medical Service are recorded in the published army lists, IOR: L/MIL/17/2–4: *Bengal* from 1819; *Madras* from 1829; *Bombay* from 1832. Dates of birth of Apothecaries are given in the lists from Oct 1884

The published *Indian Army list* 1889–1947 records all members of the Subordinate Medical Department with the rank of warrant officer or above. Details include dates of birth

Lists of apothecaries appear in *Directories: Bengal from 1815; *Madras* from 1862; *Bombay* from 1832

Warrant officers of the Subordinate Medical Department appear in the *India list* 1877–95

Senior members of the department who were employed as Civil Surgeons are recorded in Histories of Service 1875–1955, IOR: V12 – *see* p 10

War services of members of the Madras Subordinate Medical Department appear in the *Madras Army list* from 1861 to 1895, IOR: L/MIL/17/3, and all-India is covered in the *Indian Army list* Oct 1889–Jul 1919 (Jan & Jul issues only from Jul 1904) and *Indian Army list supplements* Jan 1902–Jan 1942

For furlough books 1825–1947, ie records of payments made to Subordinate Medical Service officers while on leave in the UK, *see* the series

IOR: L/AG/20/9 (1825–1939) and L/AG/20/6 (1939–47)

For records of service pensions paid to retired officers in the UK 1825–1968, *see* the series IOR: L/AG/21/11 & 13. It should be noted, however, that few Subordinate Medical Officers retired to the UK

Officers of the ISMD admitted to pension in India, 1883–1914 *see* L/AG/26/14/2–4, *ditto* wives and children, 1883–1908, L/AG/26/15/2–4

The note on Military Wills etc p 17 above applies also to Officers of the Subordinate Medical Services

FAMILY INFORMATION

See the general sources listed on pp 11–12

The only official fund applicable to the Subordinate Medical Service was the Lord Clive Fund, set up in 1770. It provided benefits for retired warrant officers and their widows, but not children. For lists of pensioners, payment books, etc, *see* the series IOR: L/AG/23/2 & L/AG/21/10

For pensions paid to widows and children of ISMD officers in the UK 1950–55 *see* IOR: L/AG/21/13/99

Indian Army Nursing Services, Voluntary Aid Detachments, and Women's Auxiliary Corps

INDIAN ARMY NURSING SERVICES

Appointments are recorded in IOR: L/MIL/9/ 430–32, Registers of Candidates 1887–1920, which give address, date of birth, date of appointment, etc. Each volume is indexed. The complementary series of application papers forms Military Collection 262A, IOR: L/MIL/7/11617–803. An index to them is inserted in IOR: L/MIL/9/430

Members of the Indian Army Nursing Services with the rank of Nursing Sister and above are recorded in the *Indian Army list* from Apr 1891. Staff Nurses are recorded from Oct 1926

There are release leave accounts and records of the payment of gratuities to members of the Indian Army Nursing Services released in the UK 1946– 47 in IOR: L/AG/20/39/1

For service pensions paid to retired members of the Indian Military Nursing Service in the UK 1950–55 *see* IOR: L/AG/21/13/97

NB From 1927 there were three Military Nursing Services in India: Queen Alexandra's Imperial Military Nursing Service, Queen Alexandra's Military Nursing Service for India, and the Nursing Service for Indian Troops' Hospitals (later called the Indian Military Nursing Service)

VOLUNTARY AID DETACHMENTS

Recruited in the UK for service in India during the Second World War

Records of service for nurses of the Voluntary Aid Detachments can be found in IOR: L/MIL/14, Personal Files. These files are not normally available to the public, but career information from them can be supplied upon request

There are release leave accounts and records of the payment of gratuities to VADs released in the UK 1946–47 in IOR: L/AG/20/41/5–6. There is also a series of payment books on appointment, 1944– 45, IOR: L/AG/20/41/1–4

WOMEN'S AUXILIARY CORPS

Officers of the Women's Auxiliary Corps are recorded in the *Indian Army list* Apr 1943–Aug 1947

There are records of service for officers and other ranks in IOR: L/MIL/14. These files are not normally available to the public, but career information from them can be supplied upon request

There are release leave accounts and records of the payment of gratuities to officers and other ranks released in the UK 1946–47 in IOR: L/AG/20/38/ 1–2. Release leave accounts for members of the Women's Auxiliary Corps (Burma) 1946–47 can be found in IOR: L/AG/20/40/1

Chaplains appointed by The East India Company 1600–1858, and The India Office 1858–1947

RECORDS OF APPOINTMENT

Early records of the appointment of chaplains in India can be found in the Court Minutes IOR: B, Committee of Correspondence records IOR: D, General Correspondence IOR: E, Factory Records IOR: G, and Proceedings IOR: P. Correspondence and proceedings relating to the Madras Presidency 1670–1760 have been published* in extenso, with indexes, by the Madras Government. There are indexes to Despatches to Bengal, Madras and Bombay 1753–1858, IOR: Z/E/4/1–72.

For the nineteenth and twentieth centuries see Court Minutes to 1853 IOR: B, Committee of Correspondence records to 1834 IOR: D, Minutes of the Political and Military Committee 1834–59 IOR: L/MIL/1/49–74, Public and Judicial Home Correspondence 1855–79 IOR: L/P & J/2, Ecclesiastical Correspondence with India 1814–79 IOR: L/P & J/3, Public and Judicial Department papers 1880–1946 IOR: L/P & J/6–7, and Services and General Department Collections 1924–48 IOR: L/S & G/7

Chaplains sometimes appear in the series of bonds for EIC officials 1771–1862, IOR: 0/1/1–145, index IOR: Z/O/1/1–2. These give the date of appointment and the names and addresses of two sureties

RECORDS OF SERVICE - COMPILATIONS

Biographical notes on the East India Company's chaplains to 1858, S J McNally (IOR, 1976, manuscript) – a continuation to 1947 is in progress

Parochial annals of Bengal, Henry Barry Hyde (Calcutta, 1901)

The Church in Madras, Frank Penny, 3 vols (London, 1904–22) IOL: V8262

Personal Records *c*1794–*c*1841 IOR: 0/6/1–20, a series of memoranda prepared at East India House, including records of service and notes on chaplains. Each volume has an index and there is also a cumulative index, IOR: Z/0/6/1–2

Histories of Service for Madras chaplains appear in the *Madras Asylum Press almanac* from 1873

Histories of Service 1875–1955, IOR: V/12, arranged by province and department. Up to *c*1930 the histories of service of chaplains are to be found mainly in the provincial series. For the period 1931–1941 consult the All-India series, V/12/22–25

Short records of service of Bishops and archdeacons are given in the *India Office list* from 1886. Senior and junior chaplains are recorded from 1927

Part II of *A list of inscriptions on Christian tombs or monuments in the Punjab (including Delhi), North-West Frontier Province, Kashmir and Afghanistan,* Miles Irving (Lahore, 1910), contains detailed biographical articles on all chaplains whose monumental inscriptions *c*1800–*c*1905 are noted in Part I

OTHER SERVICE RECORDS

Apart from Factory Records IOR: G, and the various series of Proceedings IOR: P, chaplains are recorded in the half-yearly lists of establishments in Bombay Public Proceedings 1712–93. IOR: 0/6/37 is a typescript copy of these lists 1712–52

There are notes on chaplains in India during the seventeenth and eighteenth centuries in IOR: H/ 59, 78, 360 & 803, Home Miscellaneous Series

Chaplains in all three Presidencies are recorded in the printed *list of EIC Civil Servants for 1771,1774, 1776, 1780, 1782, 1790, 1795 & 1799, in a separate printed* list of EIC Civil Servants for 1785, and in the *Bengal calendar* for 1792

Bengal chaplains are recorded in the separate printed *Bengal civil and military list* 1784–85 & 1787, and in the *Bengal calendar* 1789–90 & 1792

Annual or half-yearly lists of chaplains appear in the *East India register* 1800–60, the *Indian Army and Civil Service list* 1861–76, the *India list* 1877–1906, the *India Office list* 1907–37, and the *India and Burma Office list* 1938–40

There are lists of chaplains in the *Bengal Army list* 1839–89, *Madras Army list* 1823–95, *Bombay Army list* 1823–95, IOR: L/MIL/17/2–4, and *Indian Army list* 1889–1947. In addition to the regular chaplains of the Church of England and Church of Scotland, Wesleyan chaplains are recorded in the *Indian Army list* from Oct 1912 and United Board chaplains from Oct 1929

IOR: L/F/10, annual lists of civil servants giving details of postings and salary, record Bengal chaplains from 1829, Madras and Bombay chaplains from 1842

Civil Lists 1840–1957, IOR: V13, annual or half-yearly lists of civil establishments, arranged by province or department, include members of the ecclesiastical establishment

For furlough books 1795–1955, ie records of payments made to chaplains while on leave in the UK, *see* the series IOR: L/AG/20/12, L/AG/20/7 & L/AG/20/1

For records of service pensions paid to retired chaplains in the UK 1825–1968, which sometimes give addresses, *see* the series IOR: L/AG/21/16 (1825–1931) and L/AG/21/9 (1940–68)

FAMILY INFORMATION

See the general sources listed on pp 11–12

Chaplains received benefits from the Lord Clive Fund and were contributors to the other six military funds – *see* pp 17–18

Indian Officers and Other Ranks of The East India Company's Armies 1708–1861, and The Indian Army 1861–1947

Apart from a small number of files covering the Second World War period in IOR: L/MIL/14, the India Office Records do not contain personal records of service for Indian officers. There are no records of recruitment or service for Indian other ranks

The *Madras Army list*, IOR: L/MIL/17/3, records the names of Subadar Majors of cavalry and infantry regiments from Dec 1831

Complete lists of the Indian officers of each regiment appear in the *Bengal Army list* from Oct 1876 IOR: L/MIL/17/2, the *Madras Army list* from Mar 1877 IOR: L/MIL/17/3, the *Bombay Army list* from Jan 1877 IOR: L/MIL/17/4 and the *Indian Army list* 1889–1947. War services of Indian officers are recorded in the *January* editions of the *Indian Army list* 1890–1919 and in its *Supplements* Jan 1902–Jan 1942

The various Army Lists record the following awards to Indian officers and other ranks:
Order of British India (officers only)
Bengal Army List, by regiment from Dec 1838 and separately from Jan 1864
Madras Army List, from Jan 1842
Bombay Army List, from Apr 1851
*Indian Army List, Oct 1889–Jul 1919 (but *not* in Apr & Oct editions after Apr 1904)
*Indian Army List Supplements, Jan 1902–Jan 1942

Indian Order of Merit
Bengal Army List, from Mar 1883
Madras Army List, from Jan 1876
Bombay Army List from Jul 1890
*Indian Army List Oct 1889–Jul 1919 (but *not* in Apr & Oct editions after Apr 1904)
*Indian Army List Supplements Jan 1902–1942
Deeds of valour of the Indian Soldier which won the Indian Order of Merit during the period from 1837 to 1859, comp P.P. Hypher (Simla, 1925) IOL: T35367

Indian Distinguished Service Medal
*Indian Army List, Jan & Jul editions from Jul 1907 to Jul 1919

*Indian Army List Supplements, Jan 1920–Jan 1931
Awards to Indian officers and other ranks which are not noted in the Army Lists may often be found in the *Gazette of India*, IOR: Official Publications, and in *Indian Army General Orders*, IOR: L/MIL/17/5

The following records in the Accountant-General's Department include references to Indian officers and other ranks and their families:
IOR: L/AG/26/11/1 Pensions of Indian troops charged to the UK government 1834–87
IOR: L/AG/26/11/2 Extraordinary pensions granted to Indian troops and their dependants 1902–11
IOR: L/AG/26/17/1–2 Schedules of disability pensions awarded to Indian troops 1921–41, index IOR: L/AG/26/17/3
IOR: L/AG/26/17/4–8 Schedules of awards of pensions to dependants of Indian troops 1921–41, index IOR: L/AG/26/17/9

For payments of pensions to Indian soldiers in the Colonies/Dominions, 1907–1955 *see* L/AG/21/44/12–14

Bandsmen of the East India Company's Armies 1708–1861, and The Indian Army 1861–1947

Bandsmen attached to Indian cavalry and infantry regiments were nearly always Eurasians. There are no records of recruitment or service for them, but they were often the sons or grandsons of European soldiers (*see* p 21). For family information *see* the general sources listed on pp 11–12

Members of the bands of the Viceroy and of the Presidency Governors were European NCOs on the Unattached List and they are recorded in Bengal Unattached Lists 1866–1907 IOR: L/MIL/ 10/205–52, Bombay Unattached Lists 1896–1907 IOR: L/MIL/12/269–80, and Indian Army Unattached Lists 1908–39, IOR: L/MIL/14/ 144–74

British Army in India: Officers, Other Ranks, Medical Service and Veterinary Corps

In general the service records of officers and other ranks of British Army regiments stationed in India must be sought at the Public Record Office, Kew (to 1900) and at the Army Records Centre, Bourne Ave, Hayes, Middlesex. *See *Guide to the Public Record Office* (London, 1963) vol 2 pp 304–34

OFFICERS

The India Office Records has long runs of the various British Army Lists 1786–1949 in the Military Department Library, IOR: L/MIL/17/1

There are records of service in IOR: L/MIL/14 for certain categories of officer (eg Royal Engineers) who elected for continuous service on the Indian Establishment. Mainly from the Second World War period, they are not normally available to the public, but information from them can be supplied upon request

Lists of the officers of British Army regiments in India appear in the series Military Statements for Bengal 1785–1858, Madras 1794–1858 and Bombay 1791–1858, IOR: L/MIL/8

IOR: L/MIL/15/1–4, regimental lists of British Army units serving in India 1806–65. They contain details of promotion, leave, transfer, retirement and death for each officer, and they also provide information on the movements of regiments within India

Lists of British Army officers and details of regimental moves are given (with a few exceptions) in the *Bengal Army list* 1819–89 IOR: L/MIL/17/2, the *Madras Army list* 1810–95 IOR: L/MIL/17/3, and the *Bombay Army list* 1823–95 IOR: L/MIL/17/4. The *Indian Army list* records officers and regimental moves from 1889 to 1947

Lists of British Army officers and regimental moves also appear in the *India list* 1877–95, the *Bengal directory* from 1814, the *Bombay directory* from 1806, and the *Madras almanac* for

1800. From 1815 to 1837 the *Bengal directory* lists officers stationed in all three Presidencies

War services of British Army officers are recorded in:
Bengal, Madras and Bombay Army lists from about 1855 to 1895, IOR: L/MIL/17/2–4
Hart's annual army list 1840–1914 & Quarterly army list 1858–83, IOR: L/MIL/17/1
*Indian Army lists & supplements from 1889

For records of the furlough and duty pay of officers of British regiments serving in India 1872–1943 *see* IOR: L/AG/20/15/1–17

Other records relating to the services of British Army officers in India can be found in the series IOR: L/MIL/15/5–48 & L/AG/20/15–37

For family information *see* the general sources listed on pp 11–12

Pensions of British Army officers (Non-Effective Account) 1870–1938, *see* IOR: L/AG/26/7
Pensions to widows and orphans of British Army Officers 1870–1931, *see* IOR: L/AG/26/8

British Army officers who elected for continuous service on the Indian Establishment contributed to the Indian Military Service Family Pension Fund (1873–1914) and the Indian Military Widows' and Orphans' Fund (1915–43), *see* p 18

Honours, medals and awards *see* p 53

OTHER RANKS

Before 1860 a few NCOs of British Army regiments in India were recruited to the EIC Town Major's List and were then able to rise to warrant or departmental rank. After 1860 appointments to the Indian Army Unattached List (which replaced the Town Major's List) were made solely from among NCOs of British Army regiments *see* pp 19, 21

IOR: L/AG/26/9/2–14 Chelsea Pension Accounts 1870–1942, lists of soldiers admitted to pension, giving unit, age, total service and period of service in India, with partial index

IOR: L/AG/26/16/1–42 Lists of Chelsea Out-Pensions drawn in India 1873–1914

For records of furlough and duty pay of British Army other ranks serving in India 1889–1939 *see* the series IOR: L/AG/20/16

IOR: L/MIL/15/41–48 Records of passages of British troops from the UK to India 1868–1914. IOR: L/MIL/15/42–46 give the date of enlistment and present age of soldiers

Other records relating to the services of British Army other ranks in India can be found in the series IOR: L/MIL/15/22–37 & L/AG/20/18–25

L/MIL/15/23–26 British enlisted men transferred to the Indian Establishment, 1859–61. An index is now available in the Catalogue Hall

For family information *see* the general sources listed on pp 11–12

For family information *see* the general sources listed on pp 11–12

Honours, medals and awards *see* p 53

ARMY MEDICAL SERVICE AND VETERINARY CORPS

In 1898 the Army Medical Service became the Royal Army Medical Corps, and in 1919 the Army Veterinary Corps was also styled 'Royal'

Commissioned officers in the medical services of the British Army 1660–1960, Alfred Peterkin & William Johnstone & Robert Drew, 2 vols (London, 1968), contains biographical notes on all British Army medical officers

Regular lists of British Army medical officers in India appear in the Bengal, Madras and Bombay Army Lists from 1862/3, IOR: L/MIL/17/2–4, and in the *Indian Army list* 1889–1947

Regular lists of British Army veterinary officers in India appear in the *Bengal Army List* from Jul 1877, the *Madras Army list* from Jul 1874, the *Bombay Army list* from 1862, L/MIL/17/2–4, and the *Indian Army list* 1889–1947

IOR: L/MIL/15/20 Register of British medical officers serving in India 1872–1912, giving rank, date of embarkation, position held and station where serving, with index

IOR: L/MIL/15/21 Register of British veterinary officers on the Indian Establishment 1871–1913, giving rank and date of appointment, with index

Royal Indian Air Force and Royal Air Force in India

There is a complete set of the *Air Force List* Dec 1918–Oct 1948 in the Military Department Library, IOR: L/MIL/17/10/1–300

The IOR has a set of the Royal Indian Air Force List, 1941–1946, L/MIL/17/10/301–09

IOR: L/AG/20/47/1–10 & L/AG/20/35/1–2 Pay accounts of RIAF officers in the UK 1918–42 & 1943–47

IOR: L/AG/26/12 Nominal index of RAF personnel serving in India 1919–39

IOR: L/AG/20/36/1–6 Pay accounts of RAF officers from India serving in the UK 1943–45

IOR: L/AG/20/37/1–3 Unrecovered balances of pay of RAF officers from India serving in the UK 1943–50

Bombay Marine/Indian Navy 1613–1863

The Bombay Marine was the fighting navy of the East India Company in Asian waters, as opposed to its mercantile marine (for which *see* pp 38–39). In 1830 the Marine was renamed the Indian Navy. The Navy was abolished in 1863, being replaced by a revived, non-combatant, Bombay Marine

RECORDS OF APPOINTMENT

Records of appointment can be found in Bombay Factory Records IOR: G/3, Bombay Proceedings IOR: P, Minutes of the Committee of Shipping 1802–34 IOR: L/MAR/1/1–22, Minutes of the Finance and Home Committee 1834–59 IOR: L/F/1/1–52 indexes Z/L/F/1/1–47, and Reports of the Finance and Home Committee (Marine Branch) 1837–62 IOR: L/F/1/100–16

IOR: L/MAR/C/689 Appointment of volunteer cadets to the Bombay Marine 1794–1830. A cadet's county of origin is occasionally recorded

IOR: L/MAR/C/688 List of appointments to the Bombay Marine 1822–32. Baptismal certificates are attached in many cases, and a card index is available

IOR: L/MAR/C/710–14 Cadet papers of volunteers appointed to the Indian Navy 1838–59. They include baptismal certificates, and each volume is indexed

For other records of appointment *see* IOR: L/MAR/8/4; L/MAR/C/715–17

RECORDS OF SERVICE

History of the Indian Navy (1613–1863), Charles Rathbone Low, 2 vols, (London, 1877), includes quite detailed accounts of individual services

For the early period reference must be made to the Bombay Factory Records IOR: G/3, and Bombay Proceedings IOR: P

Lists of officers and sailors appear in Bombay Muster Rolls between 1738 and 1779, IOR: L/MIL/12/118–21 & 126–29

IOR: 0/5/31 'Bombay Inhabitants' Vol 5, records officers and sailors Dec 1764–Jan 1767

IOR: H/149 ff 157–61 lists Europeans in the Bombay Marine in Apr 1780

IOR: L/MAR/C Marine Miscellaneous Series, contains establishment records (including casualty lists and records of estates):
The main establishment lists for officers of the Bombay Marine/Indian Navy are:—
   1767–1837 L/MAR/C/680
   Jan 1844–Jul 1853 L/MAR/C/707
   Oct 1853–Jan 1860 L/MAR/C/708
   Apr 1860–Jan 1863 L/MAR/C/709
IOR: L/MAR/C/778 contains detailed records of service for Indian Navy officers 1838–48

Sailors 1766–1863, IOR: L/MAR/C/680A,681,686,690,690A,698–700, 719–31,745–51,763 & 857–62. Some records give age and county of origin

Engineers 1818–66, IOR: L/MAR/C/690,709, 732–44

Captains' clerks 1848–60, IOR: L/MAR/C/717–18. They are also recorded in lists of officers

There is a list of Bombay Marine officers in the *Bengal calendar* for 1792, and annual or bi-annual lists of officers appear in the *East India register* 1800–63, which also records pursers from Jun 1836 and captains' clerks from 1848

Lists of officers from 1806, and pursers and captains' clerks from 1829, appear in the *Bombay directory*

For records of leave and duty pay of officers in the UK 1797–1876 *see* the series IOR: L/AG/20/13

For records of service pensions paid to retired officers in the UK 1797–1933, which sometimes give addresses, *see* the series IOR: L/AG/21/21

See the general sources listed on pp 11–12. Some officers served in the Bengal and Madras Presidencies and information can therefore be found in non-Bombay records

Indian Navy Fund Established 1 Jan 1830, closed 1862, open to commissioned officers, pursers, midshipmen and clerks

IOR: L/AG/23/18/2–3 Family registers, compiled *c*1855 & Jun 1864, information provided includes ages and dates of marriage and death of subscribers, ages and dates of death of wives, dates of birth of children. The registers also state where a subscriber was married and where each of his children was born

For payment books 1864–1968, which sometimes give addresses, *see* the series IOR: L/AG/21/38

Royal Indian Marine / Navy

In 1877 the revived Bombay Marine and the Bengal Marine were combined to form HM Indian Marine, which became the Royal Indian Marine in 1892 and the Royal Indian Navy in 1935

RECORDS OF APPOINTMENT

Appointments can be traced in Military Department Correspondence IOR: L/MIL/3, Military Department Papers IOR: L/MIL/6, and Military Department Collections IOR:L/MIL/7

RECORDS OF SERVICE

Post 1863 Bombay Marine IOR: L/MAR/C/691–94 & 696–97

Bengal Marine 1821–74 IOR: L/MAR/8/12–20; L/MAR/C/762–63 *see also* Pilot Services, p 37

The Military Department Library, IOR: L/MIL/17/9, has an official *Bombay Marine list* covering 1870–77, and thereafter annual official lists for the Indian Marine, Royal Indian Marine and Royal Indian Navy 1878–1948

Lists of Bombay Marine staff appear in the *Bombay almanac* 1865–67 and in the **Times of India directory* 1864–77, IOL: ST 1205. The latter has a variable amount of information on HM Indian Marine 1878–85, but contains detailed lists of staff 1886–1941

IOR: L/MIL/16/1–9 Detailed records of service for RIM, and RIN staff *c*1840–*c*1947. They include European/Eurasian clerks, engineers and seamen as well as officers. The first five volumes give each person's date and place of birth and they also record any previous service in the Bombay or Bengal Marine Departments. An index is now available in the Catalogue Hall

IOR: L/MIL/16/10 *et seq* Personal files of officers of the RIN and RIN Volunteer Reserve during the Second World War. These files are not normally available to the public, but information from them can be supplied upon request

For records of leave and duty pay to RIM/RIN officers 1886–1950 *see* the series IOR:L/AG/20/13

For release leave accounts and records of the payment of gratuities to RIN and RINVR officers released in the UK 1945–47 *see* the series IOR: L/AG/20/13/37–45

For records of service pensions paid to retired RIM/RIN officers in the UK 1886–1968, which sometimes give addresses, *see* the series IOR: L/AG/21/21 & L/AG/21/11

IOR: L/AG/26/14/1 is a list of RIM officers admitted to pension in India 1898–1913

FAMILY INFORMATION

See the general sources listed on pp 11–12

RIM and RIN officers contributed to the Indian Military Service Family Pension Fund (1893–1914) and the Indian Military Widows' and Orphans' Fund (1915–43). For a note on these records *see* p 18

IOR: L/AG/26/15/1 is a list of widows and children of RIM officers admitted to pension in India 1898–1913

Pilot Services

RECORDS OF APPOINTMENT

IOR: L/MAR/C/689 Appointment of Volunteer
Cadets to the Bengal and Bombay Pilot Services
1794–1830. County of origin is recorded in some
cases

IOR: L/MAR/C/688 Appointments to the
Bombay Marine and Bombay Pilot Service 1822–
32. Baptismal certificates are occasionally
attached

IOR: L/MAR/8/1–3 Nominations to the
Bengal Pilot Service 1818–61, Birth/baptismal
certificates are included and each volume is
indexed

IOR: L/MAR/8/4 Appointments to the Bengal
Pilot Service 1858–61

Later recruitment details can be found in the
papers of the Revenue Department 1880–1924,
IOR: L/E/6–7. In 1924 recruitment was taken over
by the High Commissioner for India and the
papers have not survived

RECORDS OF SERVICE

Lists of pilots, masters and mates on the Bengal
Marine Establishment appear in the *Bengal
calendar* for 1790 & 1792

IOR: L/MAR/8/6–7 Lists of volunteers for the
Bengal Pilot Service 1796–1858, in alphabetical
order, with dates of promotions

IOR: L/MAR/8/5 Lists of rank of volunteers
1838–61

IOR: L/MAR/8/8–11 Lists of Bengal Pilot Service
employees 1793–1880

Notes on the Bengal Pilot Service 1838–79,
compiled by George Boddington Stuart, IOR:
MSS Eur B 274

Annual or bi-annual lists of pilots, masters and
mates on the Bengal Marine Establishment appear
in the *East India Register* 1800–03 & 1814–60, the

Indian Army and Civil Service list 1871–76, the
India list 1877–1906, the *India Office list* 1907–
37, and the *India and Burma Office list* 1938–40

Lists of pilots, masters and mates also appear in
the *Bengal directory* from 1863 and *Thacker's
Indian directory* from 1885

Annual or bi-annual lists of the Bengal Pilot
Establishment appear in the *Bengal civil list* 1864–
1942, IOR: V13

Covenanted pilots are included in the Bengal
Histories of Service 1896–1926 and in Indian
Finance Department History of Service Jul 1947,
IOR: V12
These give dates of birth and details of postings
and leave

For records of leave and duty pay of pilots in the
UK 1814–1950 *see* the series IOR: L/AG/20/13

For records of service pensions paid to retired
pilots in the UK 1814–1968, which sometimes give
addresses, *see* the series IOR: L/AG/21/21 &
L/AG/21/11

FAMILY INFORMATION

See the general sources listed on pp 11–12

For Bengal Pilot Fund pensions paid in UK 1920–
1968 *see* L/AG/21/9/151–57

East India Company's Mercantile Marine 1600–1834

See the ** List of marine records of the late East
India Company* (London, 1896). This is currently
being revised, and completed sections may be
consulted upon application to the Staff Counter in
the Catalogue Hall

Voyages of EIC ships 1605–1856 by Anthony and
Judith Farrington. Gives the physical
specifications of each ship, where known, the
name of the Principal Managing Owner, and
details of each voyage, giving the names of officers
and ports of call, and noting the existence of crew
lists/passenger lists, etc

RECORDS OF APPOINTMENT

The appointment of the officers of East Indiamen
can be traced in Court Minutes IOR: B, and
Committee of Shipping Minutes 1802–34 IOR:
L/MAR/1/1–22

IOR: L/MAR/C/669–70 Certificates of age or
baptism of various marine officers appointed
c1780–1820, with indexes

IOR: L/MAR/C/671 Baptismal certificates of
various midshipmen appointed 1820–30

IOR: L/MAR/C/687 Certificates of birth and
baptism of midshipmen appointed c1815–31

IOR: L/MAR/C/644 List of applications from
officers of the Company's own ships 1736–1810

IOR: L/MAR/C/672–73 Nominal lists of surgeons
and surgeons' mates 1801–33, recording
appointments to ships

RECORDS OF SERVICE

The journals and logs of the voyages of East
Indiamen, IOR: L/MAR/A 1605–1701, IOR:
L/MAR/B 1702–1834, frequently contain lists of
the ships' companies, although many logs are
missing for the earlier period. The wage ledgers
and receipt books, which generally accompany the

logs from 1702, give complete lists of officers and
crews

* Register of the East India Company's shipping,
Charles Hardy (London, 1799 plus editions of
1811,1813,1820 & 1835), gives the covering dates
of each voyage, the captain's name 1708–59, and
from 1760 the captain, 1st–4th officers, surgeon
and purser, with nominal indexes from 1790

IOR: L/MAR/C/651 Register of commanders in
the Company's service 1737–1832, with dates of
resignation or death

IOR: L/MAR/C/652–66 Descriptions of
commanders and officers 1771–1833, giving details
of previous service, with indexes

IOR: L/MAR/C/667 List of commanders, officers
and other ranks down to carpenters in the
Company's service Aug 1828–34, with age, service,
dates of discharge etc

IOR: L/MAR/C/649 Nominal list of commanders
and officers of the Company's own ships 1796–
1828

IOR: L/MAR/C/650 Descriptions of commanders
and officers of the Company's own ships 1815–32,
with details of service

IOR: L/MAR/C/774–77 Records of service of
masters and mates of extra ships 1796–1833, with
indexes

IOR: L/MAR/C/668 Nominal list of masters and
mates of extra ships 1796–1825

For records of compensation pensions paid to
retired officers and seamen of the Company's
mercantile marine 1809–91 *see* IOR: L/MAR/C/
789–841 & 843–54, and IOR: L/AG/21/22/1–6

IOR: L/MAR/C/849–50 Statements of service,
compiled in 1834, of EIC Mercantile Marine
commanders, officers, surgeons, pursers,
boatswains, carpenters and gunners, often
including details of marriage and births of
children. Applies only to persons still serving in
1834. An index is now available

Officers and crews of East Indiamen did not normally reside in India for any length of time, and so information is only occasionally obtainable from the general sources listed on pp 11–12

Poplar Fund Under certain conditions officers and seamen, and their families, received pensions from the Poplar Fund. For its records 1788–1893 *see* IOR: L/MAR/C/779–841 & 851–54, and IOR: L/AG/21/7/1–18. The main series of application papers, which contain a great deal of family information, are to be found at L/MAR/C/789–840, indexed at L/MAR/C/785–86. They cover the years 1809–1838

Passages to India

Ships' logs, IOR: L/MAR/B, often contain lists of both outward and homeward bound passengers

Lists of the passengers on ships calling at St Helena (mostly homeward bound) are recorded in the St Helena Public Consultations, IOR: G/32

Lists of passengers to India, recorded in the East India Company Letter Books, 1626–1753, E/3/84–111, can be located through the index to that series

The main series of official Gazettes [V/11] commences in 1831/32 and contains regular lists of passengers arriving at or departing from Calcutta, Madras and Bombay. Information on passengers in the newspapers prior to 1831 is only intermittent at best

Until 1833 permission to proceed to India had to be obtained from the Court of Directors. Court Minutes IOR: B, and Despatches IOR: E, sometimes give the name of the ship

There are lists of the arrivals and departure of passengers at Calcutta, Madras and Bombay in the *Bengal directory 1815–59, the *Madras almanac 1811–61 and the *Bombay directory 1817–56. It should be noted that some of the gaps in the sequence of Bengal Directories are covered by the Madras Directories, which also record passengers proceeding to and from Bengal

IOR: L/MAR/C/887 List of passengers to and from India in various ships 1838–45

IOR: L/MAR/C/888 Register of deposits on account of native servants accompanying passengers to England 1838–58

Names of civil and military passengers appear in payment volumes for individual passages to India 1852–1952, IOR: L/AG/24/21/1–11

For passages of soldiers see also IOR: L/MIL/9/85–106 & L/MIL/15/38–48

Law Officers, Advocates, Attornies, etc

Judges in this section should not be confused with Covenanted or Uncovenanted Civil Servants who exercised judicial functions (for which *see* pp 10, 13)

Lists of judges, advocates and attornies in Calcutta are recorded in the *India calendar* 1789 and the *Bengal calendar* 1790 & 1792

Lists of judges, law officers, advocates, attornies, proctors and solicitors appear in the *East India register* 1800–60, the *Indian Army and Civil Service list* 1861–76, and the *India list* 1877–95. Only judges and law officers are recorded in the *India list* and its successors from 1896, but there are full lists of lawyers in *Thacker's Indian directory* from 1885

Judges and law officers are included in the establishment lists from 1830 IOR: L/F/10, and in the published Civil Lists 1840–1957, IOR: V13

Judges and law officers appear in the published Provincial Histories of Service 1875–1948, IOR: V12. These give dates of birth and details of postings, leave etc

For appointments of judges to High Courts, Executive Councils, Federal Court of India and Judicial Committee of the Privy Council, 1922–48, *see* IOR: L/P & J/8/102–14

Records of pensions granted to retired judges of Supreme Courts in India can be found in the series IOR: L/AG/21/6

For family information *see* the sources listed on p 11–12

Railway Staff

The early railways in India were privately owned and managed. Later most came under state ownership and were either managed by the state or leased back to private management, while after 1925 most were both owned and managed by the state

State Railways in this context means railways owned and managed by the British Indian Government, *not* railways of Princely States

Virtually all of the 'agreements with staff' mentioned in this list are in fact contracts of appointment made in the UK. A card index to them is now available

Railway employment (especially in the lower grades) was largely the preserve of Eurasians

For appointments to State Railways made in the UK 1855–1946 *see* IOR: L/F/8/1–20, indexes IOR: Z/L/F/8/1–2

Histories of Service, State Railways 1884–1953, IOR: V/12/51–52, 54–62 & 66–80, employees of privately managed railways are not included

Civil Lists, Public Works Department 1861–1904, IOR: V/13/195–213, officers and workmen of State Railways only

Civil Lists, Railway Board, Department and Ministry 1905–57, IOR:V/13/227–43, officers and workmen of State Railways and officers of privately managed railways

There are lists of State Railway employees 1884–1900 in IOR: L/F/10/229–44 and half-yearly lists of officers of the Burma Railway Company 1922–28 in IOR: L/F/10/250

Annual lists of Covenanted Railway Employees 1927–36 & 1937–47 appear in IOR: L/S & G/6/64 & 860

Lists of railway employees are given in *Bengal, Madras and Bombay directories and in *Thacker's Indian directory*

Bengal Central Railway Company
IOR: L/AG/46/4/11 List of employees 1886–96

Burma Railway Company
IOR: L/AG/46/7/17–18 List of employees 1898–1921

Calcutta and South-East Railway Company
IOR: L/AG/46/4/13 Agreements with staff 1859–66

Eastern Bengal Railway Company
IOR: L/AG/46/10/35 Agreements with staff 1862–69, and lists of staff 1879–81

East Indian Railway Company
IOR: L/AG/46/11/133–37 Agreements with staff *c*1858–1925. IOR: L/AG/46/11/138–41 Half-yearly lists of staff 1861–90 & 1911–22, giving ages from 1886

Great Indian Peninsula Railway Company
IOR: L/AG/46/12/86–88 Agreements with employees 1881–1925 and index to appointments made in the UK 1848–80

Sind (Punjab, Delhi) Railway Company
IOR: L/AG/46/17/12 Lists of staff 1868–69

South Indian Railway Company
IOR: L/AG/46/18/1–4 Agreements with staff 1891–1940

For family information *see* the general sources listed on pp 11–12

Non-Official Inhabitants

List of European inhabitants sometimes appear in Factory Records IOR: G. and Proceedings IOR: P

Applications for permission to travel to India up to 1833 are recorded in Court Minutes IOR: B, and in the records of the Committee of Correspondence IOR: D. Announcements of permission granted were made in Despatches IOR: E

Returns of non-official European inhabitants in Bengal 1793–1830, Madras 1702–1828, and Bombay 1718–92, IOR: 0/5/26–31, and *see also* IOR: L/F/10/111 for Madras 1702–16

List of Europeans and others in the English factories in Bengal at the time of the siege of Calcutta in the year 1756, Samuel Charles Hill (Calcutta, 1902)

List of European merchants, Free Mariners and Grand Jury in Calcutta, Jul 1775, IOR: H/121 pp 203–20

Lists of Europeans in Calcutta and the country districts, showing year of arrival and ship in which arrived, *Bengal calendar* 1790

There is a series of bonds for non-official Europeans proceeding to India 1800–34 IOR: 0/1/207–367, indexes IOR: Z/O/1/7–11. These give the names and addresses of two sureties

Two *Parliamentary Papers* (House of Commons 1812/13) nos 150–51) list all persons licensed to proceed to India between 1793 and 1812

Lists of European inhabitants in the Bengal, Madras and Bombay Presidencies appear in the *East India register* from 1800 to 1837

A census of the European inhabitants of the Bombay Presidency (excluding Bombay City and Island), dated, 30 March 1851, appears in Bombay General Proceedings, 3 September 1851, no 7531 [P/350/59]. It gives information on individuals, similar to what is found in the UK Census

Lists of European and Eurasian inhabitants are recorded in *Bengal directories 1814–84, *Madras directories 1800, 1803, 1811–1935, *Bombay directories 1816–1950 and *Thacker's Indian directory* 1885–1942

Numerous other directories among the Library's holdings contain useful information, for instance:
The planting directory of India and Ceylon, 1879 IOL: T10348
Planting directory of Southern India, 1896, 1924–25, 1928, 1937, 1940, 1965 IOL: ST 1447
D'Vauz's Burma pocket almanac and directory, 1886–87, 1889, 1891 IOL: ST 1403
Hyderabad almanac and directory, 1874–76 IOL: ST 1449
Lahore directory, 1923 IOL: ST 1448
Hayes's Mysore and Coorg directory, 1884–65, IOL: ST 1402
The Tenasserim and Martaban almanac and directory, 1857 IOL: ST 1430
Travancore directory, IOL: ST 1429: 1910, 1932, 1938, 1949 (1). Lists of European and American residents

Personal Records *c*1794–*c*1841, IOR: 0/6/1–20, are a series of memoranda including notes on non-official Europeans. Each volume has an index and there is a cumulative index IOR: Z/O/61–2

For family information *see* the general sources listed on pp 11–12

For family information *see* the general sources listed on pp 11–12

SPECIAL CATEGORIES

Free Mariners In addition to the sources listed above *see also* IOR: L/MAR/C/674–78

Merchants and planters *see* the commercial sections in the directories listed above

Missionaries The following lists appear in directories:
*Bengal directories Protestant missionaries from 1835, clergy of all denominations from 1837
*Madras directories Protestant missionaries from 1833, Catholic clergy from 1838
*Bombay directories Protestant missionaries from 1839, Catholic clergy from 1852

Thacker's Indian directory Clergy of all
denominations 1885–1942
The Indian missionary directory: memorial volume,
IOL: T8760, contains biographical sketches of
Protestant missionaries to 1886

ASIANS

There are lists of Asian inhabitants in *Thacker's
Indian directory* from 1887. Asians are recorded
along with Europeans in *Madras directories until
1903, after which there are separate lists. There are
separate lists of Parsee inhabitants in Bombay
directories from 1875, and of Hindu and Muslim
inhabitants from 1883. Asians also appear in the
commercial sections

For distinguished Asians *see* the biographical
dictionaries listed on p 1, and also the
confidential/political compilations in the Military
Department Library IOR: L/MIL/17, the Political
and Secret Department Memoranda and Library
IOR: L/P&S/18 & 20, and IOR: Official
Publications

Asian Christians are occasionally recorded in the
Ecclesiastical Returns IOR: N, which also include
civil marriages between Europeans and Asians

Asian inhabitants are to be found throughout the
general series of Wills and Administrations etc
[L/AG/34/27 and 29]. There is also a specific index
to Wills and Administrations for Natives of
Northern India, 1890–1900, Z/L/AG/34/11

Princely States

IOR: N, and there is also a separate series for the States 1890–1947 IOR: N/5/1–2, separate index 1923–47 IOR: Z/N/5/1

RULERS AND THEIR FAMILIES

For genealogical works on Princely families *see* the biographical dictionaries listed on p 1

Details of the accession and death of rulers of both major and minor Princely States appear in *A collection of treaties, engagements and sanads relating to India and neighbouring countries,* Charles Umpherston Aitchison, 5th edn (Calcutta, 1929–33)

Information on rulers and their families is also obtainable from the India States Administration Reports *c*1868–1945, IOR: V/10. Date coverage varies from state to state

The rulers of both major and minor Princely States appear in the lists of Asian inhabitants in *Thacker's Indian directory* from 1912

See also the confidential/political compilations in the Military Department Library IOR: L/MIL/17, the Political & Secret Department Memoranda and Library IOR: L/P&S/18 & 20, and IOR: Official Publications

ARMED FORCES

Officers of local corps which were under the control of the Government of India, eg the Hyderabad Contingent, appear in the Bengal, Madras and Bombay Army lists IOR: L/MIL/17/2–4 and the *Indian Army list*

For forces directly under the control of the Princes *see* the *Imperial Service Forces army list* 1915–46, IOR: L/MIL/17/6. Awards and decorations to Indian States Forces are recorded in the *Indian Army list*

ECCLESIASTICAL RETURNS

The Princely States are included in the general series of Ecclesiastical Returns for the Bengal, Madras and Bombay Presidencies 1698–1968

Histories of Services, V12
There are Histories of Service for the following States:—
    Hyderabad, 1879–1903, V/12/429–33
    Mysore, 1880, V/12/379

Civil Lists, V13
There are Civil Lists for the following States:—
    Hyderabad, 1875–1903, V/13/1225–32
    Mysore, 1872–87, 1911–45, V/13/1233–34, 1238–46
    Central India Agency, 1907–41, V/13/1251–61
    Western India States Agency, 1933–47, V/13/1262–66
    Kashmir Residency 1923–26, V/13/1267
    Eastern States Agency, 1934–46, V/13/1268–69

Fort Marlborough, Sumatra

For passengers proceeding from England to York Fort (1692–1714), Fort Marlborough (1714–1753), *see* the East India Company's Letter Books, E/3/92–111

Appointments to the civil service at Fort Marlborough are recorded in Court Minutes IOR: B, the records of the Committee of Correspondence IOR: D, and Despatches IOR: E

For the administrative records of Fort Marlborough/Bencoolen 1685–1825, *see* the series IOR: G/35

List of the East India Company's civil servants 1771–1799 contains the civil establishment at Fort Marlborough for 1771, 1774, 1776, 1780, 1782, 1790, 1795 & 1799, and there is a separate *list for 1785

The *Bengal calendar* for 1792 records civil servants, surgeons, military officers and monthly writers at Fort Marlborough

There are lists of civil, military and naval officers at Fort Marlborough 1706–1817 in IOR: H/24

Lists of civil establishments and of free inhabitants appear in the *East India register* 1800–1825

Baptisms, marriages and burials at Fort Marlborough 1759–1825, IOR: N/7/1, index IOR: Z/N/7/1

Lists of births, marriages and deaths at Fort Marlborough 1819–25 in the *East India register*

Wills and inventories, etc, are recorded intermittently in the Fort Marlborough Public

Consultations IOR: G/35. There is a separate series for 1766–1810, IOR: G/35/152–155, and IOR: Z/L/AG/34/23 is an index to wills entered in the Public Consultations 1729–1820

Straits Settlements, Penang (Prince of Wales Island), Singapore and Malacca

Appointments to the civil service at Penang, Singapore and Malacca are recorded in Court Minutes IOR: B, records of the Committee of Correspondence IOR: D, and Despatches IOR: E

RECORDS OF SERVICE

For administrative records 1786–1867 *see* Straits Settlements Factory Records IOR: G/34, Bengal Proceedings IOR: P, letters from and despatches to Bengal and India IOR: E, and Financial Judicial and Political correspondence in IOR: L/F, L/P & J and L/P & S. A detailed list of sources appears in the *Journal of the Malayan Branch, Royal Asiatic Society*, XXXIII (1960) IOL: ST475

Short records of service of Company and Court officials in the Straits Settlements 1805–30, L A Hall (IOR, 1976 manuscript)

There are lists of officers at Penang 1786–1824 in IOR: H/24

Lists of civil establishments at Penang appear in the *East India register* from 1801. Law officers are recorded from 1807 and European inhabitants from Aug 1809, plus separate lists for Singapore and Malacca from 1826. From *c*1840 only a few names appear, but more detailed lists can be found in the *Bengal directory* until 1863

FAMILY INFORMATION

Baptisms, marriages and burials at Penang 1799–1829 (also returns for Malacca, 1825–29) IOR: N/8/1, index IOR: Z/N/8/1

Lists of births, marriages and deaths at Penang, Singapore and Malacca 1819–33 in the *East India register*

From 1830 to 1868 returns of baptisms, marriages and burials for Penang, Singapore and Malacca, appear regularly in Bengal Ecclesiastical Returns [N/1]

Straits Settlements wills, administrations etc 1806–53. IOR: L/AG/34/32/1–2. Each volume is indexed and IOR: Z/L/AG/34/23 in an index 1826–53

Penang: accounts of deceased estates 1813–25, IOR: L/AG/34/32/3

Straits Settlements, Penang, Singapore and Malacca: inventories and accounts of deceased estates 1819–29, IOR: L/AG/34/28

For Malacca, 1685–1835, *see also* note on R/9, on p 52

China

The chronicles of the East India Company trading to China 1635–1834 Hosea Ballou Morse, 5 vols (London 1926–29)

APPOINTMENTS

Appointments to the China establishment are recorded in Court Minutes IOR: B, and in the records of the Committee of Correspondence IOR: D

RECORDS OF SERVICE

For the administrative records of the China factory 1596–1840 *see* the series IOR: G/12 & R/10

The China establishment in 1771, 1774, 1776, 1780, 1782, 1790, 1795 & 1799 appears in the *List of the East India Company's civil servants 1771–99* and there is a separate *list for 1785

It is also listed in the *Bengal calendar* for 1790 and 1792

Lists of China writers and supercargoes are given in the *East India register* 1800–34

For records of pensions paid to retired members of the China establishment *see* the series IOR: L/AG/21/6

FAMILY INFORMATION

Baptisms, marriages and burials at Macao and Whampoa 1820–34, IOR: N/9/1, index IOR: Z/N/9/1

Births, marriages and deaths at Canton are recorded in the *East India register,* Sep 1819–May 1832

St Helena

A St Helena who's who, or a directory of the island during the captivity of Napoleon, Thomas Hancock Arnold Chaplin (London, 1919) contains biographies of the leading persons on the island 1815–21

APPOINTMENTS

Appointments to the Company's civil and military establishment on St Helena are recorded in Court Minutes IOR: B, the records of the Committee of Correspondence IOR: D, and correspondence between St Helena and London IOR: E/3 & G/32

RECORDS OF SERVICE

For the administrative records of St Helena 1677–1835 *see* the series IOR: G/32

The St Helena civil establishment in 1771, 1774, 1776, 1780, 1782, 1790, 1795 & 1799 appears in the *List of the East India Company's civil servants 1771–99,* and there is a separate *list for 1785

The *Bengal calendar* for 1792 contains a list of civil and military servants on St Helena

Lists of the St Helena civil and military establishments appear in *East India register* 1800–35. The marine establishment is recorded from 1818 and lists of European inhabitants appear from Aug 1825

There are nominal rolls of the Company's troops on St Helena in the St Helena Consultations from 1741 IOR: G/32. St Helena Muster Rolls 1789–1834, IOR: L/MIL/13/1–14, record the names of officers and other ranks of the Company's Artillery and Infantry Regiments, and from Sep 1813 give details of age, country of origin and former occupation. IOR: L/MIL/13/14 contains a list of military pensioners 1834–59, and there is an alphabetical index of pensioners 1834–37 in IOR: L/MIL/13/15 (*see also* the records of the Lord Clive Fund IOR: L/AG/23/2)

FAMILY INFORMATION

Baptisms, marriages and burials on St Helena 1767–1835, IOR: N/6/1–3, index IOR: Z/N/6/1

Wills, administrations, inventories and accounts are entered in the St Helena Consultations 1706–1835 IOR: G/32, index IOR: Z/L/AG/34/24

Ceylon

Records of the East India Company's administration of Ceylon, 1795–1802, are in the series IOR: G/11. After 1802 it is necessary to turn to Colonial Office records at the Public Record Office, Kew — *see* the *Guide to the Public Record Office* Vol 2 (London, 1963) p 61

Records of births, marriages and deaths in Ceylon are held by the Registrar-General in Colombo

List of inscriptions on tombstones and monuments in Ceylon, John Penry Lewis (Colombo, 1913) covers the period *c*1600–*c*1900 and contains quite detailed biographical notes on Dutch and English residents

Aden and the Persian Gulf

For administrative records relating to Aden and the Persian Gulf *see* the series IOR: G/29, L/P & S/9, R/15 & R/20, and Bombay Proceedings IOR: P. IOR: R/15 is covered in detail in *The records of the British Residency and Agencies in the Persian Gulf*, Penelope Tuson (London, 1979)

IOR: N/13/1–21 Returns of births/baptisms, marriages and burials at Aden 1840–1969. They are to a large extent duplicated in the Bombay Ecclesiastical Returns IOR: N/3

Births, marriages and deaths at Aden are included in the Bombay Presidency returns in the *East India register* 1840–44 and *Bombay directories 1840–83 (covering together the years 1839–82)

IOR: N/12/1–16 Returns of births, marriages and deaths in the Kuwait Political Agency 1937–61

Gazetteer of the Persian Gulf, Oman and Central Arabia, John Gordon Lorimer, 4 vols (Calcutta, 1908–15), IOR: L/MIL/17/15/139, has useful lists of British and foreign diplomats etc from 1584, and genealogical trees of the ruling families

See also the confidential/political compilations in the Political & Secret Department Memoranda and Library IOR: L/P & S/18 & 20

Foreign Settlements in India and the East Indies

IOR: I/1/1–17 Records relating to the French in India 1664–1820

IOR: I/2/1–32 Records relating to the Dutch in India 1586–1824

IOR: I/3/1–106 Transcripts and translations of Dutch records at the Hague 1600–1700

IOR: I/3/107–165 Transcripts and translations of Portuguese records at Lisbon and Evora 1495–1806

The Home Miscellaneous series, IOR: H, contains many items relating to the French, Dutch, Danish and Portuguese settlements in India, especially during the eighteenth century

Quite detailed lists of the civil and military officers of the foreign settlements in India appear in the *Madras almanac 1836–62, and they also occur intermittently in the *Bengal directory and *Bombay directory

Lists of establishments at foreign settlements during periods of British occupation can be found in Proceedings, IOR: P. For example Madras Military Proceedings Sep–Oct 1793 contain complete lists of the French military and naval establishments at Pondicherry

Some tombstone inscriptions from the foreign settlements in India c1600–c1900 appear in the published *series of Monumental Inscriptions

IOR: R/9 The records of the Malacca Council of Justice and Orphan Chamber (1685–1835) contain much biographical information on European, Eurasian and Asian inhabitants, in the way of Wills, Estate Papers, etc, especially for the period, 1785–1825. The entries in the Register of Marriages, 1820–24 [R/9/39/3], have been added to the general biographical card index in the Catalogue Hall

Honours,
Medals and Awards

*Honours Records 1858–1947, Amar Kaur Jasbir Singh, (IOR, 1977 manuscript)

CIVIL

The following honours and awards are recorded in the *East India register* 1800–60, the *Indian Army and Civil Service list* 1861–76, the *India list* 1877–1906. *India Office list* 1907–37, and the *India and Burma Office list* 1938–47

Order of the Bath, Order of the Star of India, Order of St Michael and St George, Order of the Indian Empire, Royal Victorian Order, Order of the British Empire, Imperial Service Order, Order of the Crown of India, Royal Red Cross, Kaisar-i-Hind Medal

From 1920 awards other than the four specifically Indian ones are recorded in an alphabetical Honours List; the Indian orders have separate lists and also appear in the alphabetical list

Other civilian awards (eg King's Police Medal, Indian Police Medal) are recorded in the *London Gazette, Gazette of India* and the various provincial gazettes, IOR: Official Publications, and details of awards occasionally appear in Histories of Service. There is a microfilm of King's Police Medal awards 1909–47 IOR: NEG 3310, and for the Indian Police Medal *see* IOR: MSS Eur E358/2

See also IOR: L/P & S/15, Honours Correspondence 1859–1930

MIITARY

The VC and DSO, Garret O'Moore Creagh & Edith Humphris, 3 vols (London, 1924)

Bengal, Madras and Bombay Army lists IOR: L/MIL/17/2–4 and the *Indian Army list* record the following awards to officers and men:

Victoria Cross, Order of the Bath, Order of the Star of India, Order of St Michael and St

George, Order of the Indian Empire, Royal Victorian Order, Order of the British Empire, Distinguished Service Order, Kaisar-i-Hind Medal, Royal Red Cross, Military Cross, Military Medal, Distinguished Flying Cross, Air Force Cross, Distinguished Conduct Medal, Order of British India, Indian Order of Merit, Indian Distinguished Service Medal

Foreign orders and decorations awarded to Indian Army officers are also listed

For a detailed breakdown of records of awards to Indian officers and men *see* p 29

Military awards not recorded in the army lists (eg Long Service and Good Conduct medal) can be found in *General Orders,* IOR: L/MIL/17/5, and in the *London Gazette* and *Gazette of India,* IOR: Official Publications. These sources also give the citations for the awards listed above

Campaign Medals IOR: L/MIL/5/42–141, Medal Rolls, record the award of campaign medals to European officers and other ranks of the Company's Armies, the Indian Army and the British Army in India, but they do not cover all the campaigns for which medals were awarded. Indian campaign medals awarded to British Army officers and other ranks are also recorded in the Medal Rolls at the Public Record Office, Kew, *see* the *Guide to the Public Record Office* Vol 2 (London, 1963) pp 309–10. Indian officers and men only appear sporadically in the L/MIL/5 medal rolls

Campaign medals are also recorded in the War Services sections of the Bengal, Madras and Bombay army lists IOR: L/MIL/17/2–4, and the *Indian Army list*

Campaign medals are occasionally recorded in personal records of service, IOR: L/MIL/14/237 *et seq*

Prize and Batta Rolls, IOR: L/MIL/5/142–350, can confirm the presence of European officers and other ranks in a particular campaign 1793–1886

See also IOR: L/P & S/15, Honours
Correspondence 1859–1930

Some officers and men of the Bombay Marine/
Indian Navy were entitled to the East India
Company's General Service Medal 1854 – *see*
especially L/MIL/5/53, 54, 56

IOR: L/MIL/5/66, Marine Medals 1801–60, lists
of naval officers and men entitled to medals for
campaigns 1801–1860, with an index of ships

IOR: L/MAR/C/878, Naval Medal List 1843–47
for action in the Opium War of 1840–42

Honours and awards to Royal Indian Marine/
Navy personnel (eg Naval General Service Medal)
are recorded in Military Department Files and
Collections, IOR: L/MIL/6–7, and in personal
records of service, IOR: L/MIL/16

See also L/P & S/15, Honours Correspondence
1859–1930

Passport Records

Duplicate identity certificates of natives of India proceeding to Europe 1900–17 (when their issue ceased) and duplicate passports from 1907 were sent to the India Office. Identity certificates 1900–17 and passports 1907–15 are in IOR: L/P & J/6. The duplicate passports for 1916–31 appear to have been destroyed. Those returned 1932–49, mainly for Asians but including some Europeans and Eurasians, are in IOR: L/P & J/11, indexes IOR: Z/L/P & J/11/1–16. They cover Pakistan only for 1948–49

It should be noted that the series of duplicates are far from complete

Divorce Records

The India Office did not maintain a record of divorces granted in India and enquirers must refer to the provincial High Court which granted the decree. The present High Courts of India, Pakistan and Bangladesh do not make searches, but a list of lawyers in the three countries who will perform such work is available

If the decree absolute was granted under the provisions of the Indian and Colonial Jurisdictions Act 1926 (16 & 17 Geo 5 c.40), it should be registered in the Probate Division of the British High Court

Evacuees and Refugees, Internees and Parolees, 1939–1945

During the Second World War India gave refuge to some 400,000 people, most of them British nationals evacuated from the war zone. The largest single group left Burma on the Japanese invasion

IOR: M/8/57–58 Burma Evacuee Registers, compiled in 1943
Pt 1: Europeans, Eurasians and other non-Indian evacuees, also Arakanese, Burmese, Chinese and Shans known to have arrived in India, with lists of casualties
Pt 2: Indian evacuees, with lists of casualties

IOR: L/P & J/8/381–450, Political Department Collection 110 on evacuees and refugees in India, their accommodation in camps, and their eventual repatriation, 1940–50, including nominal lists and correspondence on individual cases

IOR: L/AG/40/1 Files and accounts of the evacuee and refugee camps, 1940–48. IOR: L/AG/40/1/131 gives nominal lists and references to individual cases

IOR: L/P & J/8/30–76, Political Department Collection 101, covers the administration of internment camps and parole centres for civilian enemy aliens, with correspondence about individual cases and repatriations, 1939–48. There are nominal rolls in IOR: L/P & J/8/31–33, giving date of birth, date and place of arrest, occupation, normal domicile, proposed destination and security classification

Lists of Japanese exchanged for British nationals are given in IOR: L/P & J/8/402–04, and there are lists of Japanese interned at Deoli Camp, Ajmer, in IOR: L/P & J/8/405

Following independence in 1947–48 many British subjects of European origin wished to return to the UK. All financial assistance granted by the UK High Commissioners in India, Pakistan and Burma was recoverable. Individual repatriation files c1947–c1960, are in IOR: L/AG/40/3, and nominal lists are in preparation

Index

Glossary of terms used in the administration of British India

ABBREVIATIONS

q.v.	'which see': i.e. term is defined elsewhere in Glossary
EIC	East India Company
HEICS	Honourable East India Company's (Civil) Service
ICS	Indian Civil Service
IOR	India Office Records
NCOs	Non-Commissioned Officers
VCO	Viceroy's Commissioned Officer

Note: *References to L/AG/..., L/MIL/..., etc, are to India Office Records series.*

GLOSSARY

Adalats. Courts of first instance in India administering mainly Hindu and Islamic Law. *See also* Sadr Adalat, Supreme Courts.

Addiscombe Military Seminary *(p8)* The East India Company's Military Seminary was established in January 1809 at Addiscombe Place, near Croydon. Its purpose was to provide up to two years' general and technical education for youths of between fourteen and eighteen who had been nominated for officer cadetships in the Company's forces. Attendance at Addiscombe was compulsory for artillery and engineer cadets, optional for cavalry and infantry cadets. After the demise of the Company in 1858, Addiscombe was converted into the Royal India Military College and continued to function till its closure in August 1861. *See* L/MIL/1 and 9, and L/AG/45. *See also* East India College (Haileybury).

Advocate *(p41)* The equivalent in the Indian High Courts, (as in the Scottish High Courts), of an English barrister.

Annuities *see* Civil Annuities, Medical Annuities.

Apothecary *(p25)* The title given to the various grades of warrant officer in the Indian Military Subordinate Medical Service. The rank of Apothecary was abolished in the Subordinate Medical Service in 1894 and replaced by that of

Assistant Surgeon. Apothecaries in the Indian Army undertook general medical duties – by the early 19th century the word was used in the more general sense of medical practitioner as well as in its original meaning of pharmacist.

Assistant Surgeon *(pp23-25)* Until 1873 the most junior grade in the Bengal, Madras, and Bombay Medical Services (Indian Medical Service). Abolished in the IMS in 1873 it replaced the grade of Apothecary in the Military Subordinate Medical Service in 1894.

Asylum Press Almanac *see* Madras Almanac.

Attorneys *(p41)* The equivalent in India of solicitors in the UK.

Auxiliary Force, India *(pp15-22)* From 1920 the equivalent in India of the Territorial Army in the UK, i.e. part-time regiments of European soldiers who could be fully mobilised in time of war. Prior to 1920 they were known as the Indian Volunteer Force (1857-1917) and the Indian Defence Force (1917-1920). There are no service files for either officers or other ranks but the names of officers appear in Bengal, Madras and Bombay Army Lists (L/MIL/17/2, 3, 4) and in Indian Army Lists 1889-1947 (L/MIL/17/5). The war services of AFI officers are recorded in Indian Army List Supplements from July 1922 onwards.

Bandsmen *(p30)* Members of a military band. There were two distinct categories of band:

(1) Members of the bands of the Viceroy and of the Governor of Bombay were British NCOs and private soldiers on the Unattached List. The bandmasters of these bands were usually civilians, before 1914 often musicians of German extraction.

(2) Bandsmen attached to EIC/Indian Army regiments of native cavalry and infantry were almost invariably Eurasians. In the late 18th and very early 19th century their names appear occasionally in the Bengal, Madras and Bombay Army Muster rolls but thereafter as non-combatants they are no longer included in the military records.

Note: Buglers and drummers who served with the British Army or the EIC European Artillery/ Infantry were not bandsmen but combatant soldiers.

Bengal, Madras and Bombay Civil Funds *(p12)* Provided benefits for the widows and children of members of the East India Company's Civil Service (HEICS) and the Indian Civil Service (ICS), i.e. the top general administrative cadre in India. Closed to new subscribers c1882-85. Records at IOR are mainly from late 19th century onwards: Fund registers, L/AG/23/5,8,11; Payment books, L/AG/21/25,28,31.

Bengal Military Fund *(pp17, 24, 28)* Provided benefits for the widows of regular officers, surgeons and chaplains of the East India Company's Bengal Army. Closed to new subscribers 1862. Records at IOR are mainly from mid-19th century onwards: Fund registers, L/AG/23/6; Payment books, L/AG/21/26.

Bengal Military Orphan Society *(pp17-18, 24, 28)* Provided benefits for the children (both legitimate and illegitimate) of regular officers, chaplains and surgeons of the East India Company's Bengal Army. Records at IOR are mainly mid-19th century onwards, with some earlier items: Fund registers, L/AG/23/7; Payment books, L/AG/21/27.

Board of Commissioners for the Affairs of India *(p3)* The formal title of the institution more commonly known as the Board of Control or the India Board, established by Act of Parliament in 1784 to 'superintend, direct and control' the East India Company's civil and military government and the business connected with its Indian revenues. By the Government of India Act of 1858, the powers of the Board and the Company were transferred to the Secretary of State for India in Council.

Bombay Civil Fund *see under* Bengal, Madras and Bombay Civil Funds.

Bombay Military Fund *(pp18, 24, 28)* Provided benefits for the widows and children of regular officers, surgeons and chaplains of the East India Company's Bombay Army. Closed to new subscribers 1862. Records at IOR are mainly mid-19th century onwards: Fund registers, L/AG/23/12; Payment books, L/AG/21/32.

Cadets *(pp8, 15, 34)* Junior entrants to the regular officer corps of the East India Company's Army (1760-1861), the Indian Army (1861-1947) and the Bombay Marine/Indian Navy (1794-1859).

Calendar. Published précis of original documents.

Chaplains *(pp27-28)* Clergymen of the Church of England and Church of Scotland appointed to serve as chaplains to the armed forces in India. In practice they ministered to the civilian population as well as to military personnel but they were part of the EIC/Indian Army establishment and governed by military regulations in respect of pay, leave and pensions. From the second quarter of the 19th century Catholic priests were allowed to officiate as army chaplains. They received subsidies from Government but were not part of the official establishment.

Chelsea Pensions *(pp31-32)* Pensions paid to time-expired or disabled British Army other ranks. So-called because the recipients were regarded as out-pensioners of the Royal Hospital, Chelsea. European other ranks of the EIC Army received Lord Clive Fund pensions unless they transferred to the British Army.

Chief Commissioner *(pp10-12, 15-18)* The Head of a Non-Regulation Province where the province did not have the status of a Lieutenant-Governorship.

Civil Annuities *(p11)* The term used for pensions paid to the Honourable East India Company's Civil Service (HEICS), which in 1858 became the Indian Civil Service (ICS), i.e. the top general administrative cadre in India. Private annuity funds for EIC civil servants were already in existence before 1826 but it was only in that year that the East India Company agreed to contribute to such funds for all three Presidencies. In the beginning Annuities were limited in number and dependent on a certain number of years' service. From 1835 they were paid quarterly instead of annually but they continued to be called Annuities to distinguish them from Civil Pensions. From 1871 all ICS officers were allowed to retire on £1000 per annum after 25 years total service, whatever the amount of their final salary. Annuities were non-contributory for those who joined the ICS after 1 April 1919.

Civil Pensions *(p14)* Term used for pensions paid to all retired members of the civil services of India apart from the Indian Civil Service.

Collector *(pp10-12)* Term used in the Regulation Provinces for the chief administrative official of a district. The title reflects the fact that revenue collection had always been an important part of district administration. In the Madras and Bombay Provinces the district officer usually bore the title of Collector and District Magistrate, in the other Regulation Provinces the title of Magistrate and Collector.

Commissariat *(pp15-20)* Name given in the late 18th and 19th century to the department(s) of the EIC/Indian Army responsible for procuring equipment and supplies (other than ordnance). The title changed to Commissariat and Transport Department 1887, Supply and Transport Corps 1901, Indian Army Service Corps 1923, Royal Indian Army Service Corps 1935.

Commissary *(pp19-20)* From 1904 the highest rank of Departmental Officer in the Indian Army – before 1904 the highest rank of Departmental Officer was Deputy Commissary.

Commissioned Officers *(pp15-18)* Generally used to mean King's or Queen's Commissioned Officers, i.e. regular officers of the Indian Army who received their commissions direct from the Monarch, to be distinguished from Viceroy's Commissioned Officers who received their commissions from the Viceroy of India.

Commissioner *(pp10-12, 15-18)* An officer in charge of the administration of a Division (comprising several Districts or Zillahs). In the Regulation Provinces he was always a member of the Covenanted Civil Service; in the Non-Regulation Provinces he could be either a

Covenanted Civil Servant or an officer of the EIC/Indian Army.

Conductor *(pp19-20)* The higher of the two Warrant Officer ranks in the EIC/Indian Army, the lower being that of Sub-Conductor. Conductors and Sub Conductors worked mainly in the Ordnance, Commissariat and Public Works Departments. Conductors were eligible for promotion to the higher grade of Departmental Officer.

Council of India *(p4)* The body appointed by Act of Parliament in 1858 to advise and to a certain extent control the Secretary of State for India (for a description of its powers *see* M I Moir, *Guide to the India Office Records*, pp73-80). Replaced in 1937 by the Board of Advisers to the Secretary of State for India and Burma.

Covenanted Civil Service *(pp10-12)* The name given to the top general administrative cadre of civil servants in India (until 1858 the Honourable East India Company's Civil Service, HEICS, after 1858 the Indian Civil Service, ICS). So called from the good behaviour covenants which appointees were obliged to enter into with the EIC Court of Directors, and (after 1858) with the Secretary of State for India in Council. To be distinguished both from the Uncovenanted Civil Service and from the Special Civil Services.

Dafadar *(p29)* An NCO in the Indian Cavalry equivalent in rank to a Havildar in the Indian Infantry.

Departmental Officers *(pp19-20)* These Officers were recruited from the EIC/Indian Army's Conductors and served mainly in the Ordnance, Commissariat and Public Works Departments. Prior to 1904 they held the ranks (in ascending order) of Deputy Assistant Commissary, Assistant Commissary and Deputy Commissary. In 1867 these ranks were given complementary honorary officer ranks ranging from Honorary Ensign to Honorary Captain. From 1904 Departmental Officer ranks were regraded as Assistant Commissary, Deputy Commissary and Commissary with equivalent honorary officer ranks from Honorary Lieutenant to Honorary Major. In 1921 the prefix 'Honorary' was discarded and the complementary ranks assimilated to those of regular officers.

Deputy Collector *(pp13-14)* In the Regulation Provinces a member of the Uncovenanted Civil

Service in charge of a subdivision of a district; the equivalent of an Extra Assistant Commissioner in a Non-Regulation Province (*q.v.*).

Deputy Commissioner *(pp10-12, 15-18)* In the Non-Regulation Provinces an officer in charge of the civil administration of a District; equivalent to a Magistrate and Collector in the Regulation Provinces.

Discharge Papers *(pp21-22)* Register of soldiers who took the option of unpensioned discharge when the EIC European troops were amalgamated with the British Army in 1859-61. These papers are a convenient source of biographical information since they include both the soldier's service details and a duplicate copy of his entry in the recruitment register, giving physical description, parish of origin etc. An index to the Discharge Papers is available in the OIOC Reading Room.

District Officer *(pp10-12, 15-18)* An officer in charge of the civil administration of a district. In the Regulation Provinces after 1858 he usually held either the title of Magistrate and Collector or (in the Madras and Bombay Provinces) the title of Collector and District Magistrate; in the Non-Regulation Provinces he was called Deputy Commissioner.

Diwani Adalat *see* Sadr Diwani Adalat.

East India College/Haileybury *(p8)* Established first in 1806 at Hertford Castle and transferred to Haileybury in 1809, it provided a general and vocational education for youths of sixteen to eighteen nominated by EIC Directors to writerships in the EIC overseas civil service. Attendance was generally for four terms, i.e. two years. In 1856 the system of appointment by patronage was replaced by an open competitive examination and in January 1858 the college was closed down.

Echelon. An administrative division, especially one (e.g. the Indian Imperial Police) which recruited mainly by direct appointment rather than by promotion from an inferior division.

Effective Supernumeraries *(p21)* The term used in the EIC Madras Army for what in the EIC Bengal and Bombay Armies was called the Town Major's List (*q.v.*).

Elders *(p6)* The name given to foremen of warehouses in the EIC Home Civil Service in London.

Embarkation Lists *(p21)* Registers of EIC Army recruits embarked for India, compiled at the port of embarkation. Before the commencement of the Recruitment Registers proper in 1801 they are the main source of information on recruits but the extent of information varies from register to register – some giving full personal details, others only the name and the date of joining ship. An alternative source of information on pre-1801 EIC Army recruits are the Registers of Lord Clive Fund Applications 1772-1798: L/AG/23/2/20-22.

Emergency Commissions *(pp16-17)* Commissions in the Indian Army granted to European soldiers specifically for the duration of World War II. The IOR holds service files for about 80% of these officers. Those Emergency Commissioned (EC) officers who had been in civilian life prior to the outbreak of war (the great majority) were not entitled to a pension but received a gratuity upon final discharge (*see* the series L/AG/20/29 and L/AG/20/31). A few EC officers who had seen rank service in the British Army before 1939 were entitled to a pension in respect of their combined British and Indian service. Payments of these pensions are recorded in the series L/MIL/21/14 (1950-56) and in the series L/MIL/21/11 (1956-67).

Extra Assistant Commissioner *(pp13-14)* In the Non-Regulation Provinces a member of the Uncovenanted Civil Service in charge of a subdivision of a district; the equivalent of a Deputy Collector in a Regulation Province.

Factor *(pp10-12)* The 3rd of the four classes into which the East India Company's civil servants were originally divided, the others being 1st: Senior Merchant, 2nd: Junior Merchant, 4th: Writer. The term Factor originally meant a commercial agent or the executive head of a Factory, but it continued to be used as a rank in the Company's service long after the duties of the Company's officials had ceased to be primarily commercial. It last appears as a civil service rank in the East India Register in 1841.

Factory. An EIC trading establishment in India and elsewhere.

Faujdari Adalat *see* Sadr Faujdari Adalat.

Free Mariners *(p43)* Seamen allowed by the East India Company to engage in the country trade, i.e. the local trade of South and South East Asia – the Company retained its monopoly on trade between Britain and India until 1813 and between Britain and China until 1833.

Furlough *(pp17, 20, 24-25, 28, 31-32, 34, 36-37)* Leave of absence granted to a soldier, sometimes loosely used with reference to non-military personnel instead of the more correct term civil leave.

Gazetted Posts *(pp10-18)* Posts in the Indian civil services, appointments to which were notified in the Government Gazettes – in practice this meant all posts in the Covenanted Civil Service (HEICS, ICS) and the higher posts in the Uncovenanted Civil Service and Special Civil Services. All gazetted officers were *ipso facto* recorded in the published Civil Lists (V/13) and 'Histories of Service' (V/12).

Gratuities *(pp17, 53)* One-off payments made to military personnel upon termination of service (in lieu of pension), also used at an earlier period to refer to payments made to soldiers after a campaign (in lieu of prize money).

Guaranteed Railways *(p42)* Term used to describe the eight privately financed Indian railway companies which had been formed by 1859, so-called because the Government of India guaranteed a minimum return on their capital.

Gunner *(pp21-22, 31-32)* In the EIC Artillery and Royal Artillery an ordinary artilleryman equivalent in rank to a Private in the Infantry and a Trooper in the Cavalry.

Haileybury *see* East India College.

Havildar *(p29)* In the Indian Army an Indian non-commissioned officer equivalent to a Sergeant in the British Army.

Havildar-Major *(p29)* The most senior NCO rank in the Indian Infantry equivalent to a Sergeant-Major in the British Infantry and to a Kot Dafadar in the Indian Cavalry.

High Commissioner for India *see* Indian High Commission.

High Courts *(pp10-12, 41)* Established by Act of Parliament in 1862 at Calcutta, Madras and Bombay, they amalgamated the functions of the Supreme Courts and the Sadr Courts. An additional High Court was established by Act of Parliament at Allahabad in 1866 and Chief Courts were established, by Act of the Indian Legislature, at Lahore in 1866 and at Rangoon in 1900.

Honorary Commissioned Officers *(pp19-20)* From 1867 Departmental Officers *(q.v.)* were given honorary officer ranks ranging from Honorary Ensign to Honorary Captain – these ranks were additional to their existing commissary grades. From 1904 following the regarding of their commissary ranks the complementary honorary officer ranks now ranged from Honorary Lieutenant to Honorary Major. In 1921 the prefix 'Honorary' was discarded and the complementary ranks assimilated to those of regular officers.

Honourable East India Company's Civil Service (HEICS) *(pp10-12)* Before 1858 the name given to the top general administrative cadre of civil servants in India. In 1858 it became the Indian Civil Service.

Imperial Service Troops *(p45)* Regiments raised by the Rulers of certain Princely States (1888–) and made available to the British Crown for service overseas. Officers of the Indian Army were attached to them as advisers. From 1922 known as Indian States Forces.

India High Commission *(p9)* Established in London in 1920 (not to be confused with the post-Independence India High Commission which inherited its records). It took over certain responsibilities hitherto exercised by the India Office, e.g. the Stores Department, the Indian students' advisory service, the issue of civil leave pay and pensions, etc. In February 1922 it acquired additional responsibilities including civilian steamship passages, exhibitions and the care of destitute *lascars* (Indian seamen), and from February 1924 it was responsible for recruitment to certain official posts in India.

Indian Civil Service (ICS) *(pp10-12)* The name given after 1858 to the top general administrative cadre of civil servants in India. It superseded the Honourable East India Company's Civil Service. The last UK appointments to the ICS were made in 1942. *See also* Covenanted Civil Service.

Indian Civil Service Family Pension Fund (ICSFPF) *(p12)* Established in 1881, it provided benefits for the widows and children of members of the ICS. Last subscriber joined 1942. Fund registers, L/AG/23/13; Payment books, L/AG/21/33.

Indian Commissioned Officers *(p29)* Native officers of the EIC/Indian Army (also known after 1858 as Viceroy's Commissioned Officers). In the Infantry they held the ranks of Jemadar, Subadar and Subadar-Major, in the Cavalry the ranks of Jemadar, Ressaidar, Risaldar and Risaldar-Major.

Indian Defence Force *(pp15-22)* Name given between 1917-1920 to what had formerly been known as the Indian Volunteer Force. In 1920 it became the Auxiliary Force, India.

Indian Distinguished Service Medal *(p29)* Instituted in 1907 as an award to recognise distinguished services of Indian Commissioned and Non-Commissioned Officers, extended in 1929 to the Royal Indian Marine and in 1940 to the Indian Air Force. Recipients of the IDSM are recorded in Indian Army List Supplements up to and including January 1931.

Indian Medical Service *(pp23-24, 53-54)* Collective name for the top echelon of the EIC/Indian Army's medical service. Until 1896 it was divided into three administrative divisions, *viz*: Bengal Medical Service, Madras Medical Service, Bombay Medical Service. In Jan 1897 these three services were combined into one general service under the direct administrative control of the Government of India. Up to 1891 IMS officers had medical ranks, e.g. Surgeon, Surgeon Major etc. In January 1892 these were replaced with compound ranks, i.e. medical rank plus combatant rank e.g. Surgeon Lieutenant. From September 1898 the medical titles were discarded and IMS officers had the same ranks as regular officers.

Indian Military Service Family Pension Fund (IMSFPF) *(pp18, 24, 28, 31, 36)* Established 1873, it provided benefits for the widows and children of regular officers, surgeons and chaplains of the Indian Army. Officers of the Royal Indian Marine and continuous service officers of the Royal Artillery and Engineers were allowed to subscribe from 1893. Closed to new subscribers 1914: Fund registers, L/AG/23/16; Payment books, L/AG/21/35.

Indian Military Widows' and Orphans' Fund (IMWOF) *(pp18, 24, 26, 31, 36)* Established 1915, it provided benefits for the widows and children of the following categories of officers: regular officers, surgeons and chaplains of the Indian Army, officers of the Royal Indian Marine/Navy, continuous service officers of the Royal Artillery, Royal Engineers, and Royal Army Veterinary Corps, officers of the Royal Corps of Signals, and officers transferred from the British Service to the Indian Army Ordnance Corps. Last subscriber joined 1943: Fund registers, L/AG/23/17; Payment books, L/AG/21/36.

Indian Non-Commissioned Officers (Indian NCOs) *(p29)* In the EIC/Indian Army the majority of Indian NCOs held the ranks of Lance-Naik, Naik, Havildar and Havildar-Major corresponding to the British ranks of Lance-Corporal, Corporal, Sergeant and Sergeant-Major. In the Indian Cavalry post-1858 the ranks were Lance-Dafadar, Dafadar and Kot Dafadar.

Indian Order of Merit *(p29)* Oldest gallantry award in the British Empire, introduced by the East India Company for its native troops in 1837. Originally in three classes. Was at first called the Order of Merit but the name was changed to Indian Order of Merit in 1902 to distinguish it from the newly instituted (Imperial) Order of Merit.

Indian Police (*also known as*** Indian Imperial Police)** *(pp13-14)* Name given from the 1890s to the upper echelon of the Indian Police Services. Recruited (from 1893) largely by examination in the UK. From 1921 direct appointments to the Indian Imperial Police were also made by an annual examination in India open to all races and over the next 26 years the service was progressively Indianized.

Indian States Forces (ISF) *(p45)* Title given (1922-1947) to what were previously termed Imperial Service Troops.

Indian Volunteer Force *(pp15-22)* Name given from 1857 to 1917 to what was later called the Indian Defence Force (1917-1920) and the Auxiliary Force, India (1920-1947).

Jemadar *(p29)* In the EIC/Indian Army the most junior rank of Indian Commissioned Officer, equivalent to a Lieutenant in the British Army.

Judges *(pp10-14, 41)* In British India there were a multiplicity of courts and judicial titles but it is useful to distinguish between the following four types of judge:
(1) Barristers of England or Ireland or Scottish Advocates, not members of the HEICS/ICS, appointed before 1862 to be Judges of the Supreme Courts in India, after 1862 as Judges of the High Courts in India – they served a limited number of years but were entitled to Indian Government pensions.
(2) Members of the Judicial Branch of the EIC/Indian Civil Service or of the Uncovenanted Civil Services – the great majority of judges fell into this category. Before 1862 the upper echelon served as Judges of the Adalat and Sadr Adalat Courts, after 1862 as District and Sessions Judges and Judges of the High Courts / Chief Courts. From the late 19th century onwards they were encouraged to obtain legal degrees and/or qualify as barristers. Below this upper echelon came Subordinate Judges and Munsifs.
(3) Magistrates/Collectors – partly members of the ICS and partly drawn from the Uncovenanted Service. Their duties were primarily administrative but as magistrates they exercised judicial authority in minor cases.
(4) Pleaders of the Indian High Courts not in Indian Government Service appointed after 1862 to fill a certain proportion of High Court Judgeships and District and Sessions Judgeships.

Junior Merchant *(pp10-12)* The second of the four classes into which the East India Company's civil servants were originally divided, the others being 1) Senior Merchant, 3) Factor, 4) Writer. As the name indicates it originally had a commercial significance but it continued to be used as a rank in the Company's service long after the duties of the Company's officials had ceased to be primarily commercial – it last appears as a civil service rank in the East India Register in 1841.

Kaisar-I-Hind Medal *(p53)* Instituted in 1900 to reward those who had performed useful public service in India. The 1st Class was in gold and awarded by the Sovereign on the recommendation of the Secretary of State for India, the 2nd Class was in silver and awarded by the Viceroy of India. For correspondence regarding the award and statements of service of recipients *see* the series L/P&S/15.

King's Indian Commissioned Officers *(p29)* Indians granted commissions as regular officers in the Indian Army, to be distinguished from Viceroy's Commissioned Officers *(q.v.)*. Temporary regular commissions were first granted to Indians towards the end of World War I, and about the same time a small number of Indian cadets began to be selected on an annual basis for admission to the Royal Military Academy, Sandhurst, where they were trained to become regular officers of the Indian Army.

Kot Dafadar *(p29)* The most senior NCO rank in the Indian Cavalry, equivalent to a Troop Sergeant-Major in the British Cavalry and to a Havildar-Major in the Indian Infantry.

Lance-Dafadar *(p29)* An NCO in the Indian Cavalry equivalent in rank to a Naik in the Indian Infantry.

Lance-Naik *(p29)* An NCO in the Indian Infantry equivalent in rank to a British Lance-Corporal.

Law Officer *(p41)* A Government legal official usually with general responsibilities as opposed to an officer of a particular court. In the Governments of India, Madras and Bombay the principal law officers were the Advocate General, the Government Solicitor and the Administrator General.

Letters Patent *(p3)* A document issued by the British Monarch conferring upon a person or persons some right or privilege, title, property or office.

Lord Clive Fund *also known as* **Military (Late Lord Clive) Fund** *(pp17, 20, 22, 24, 25, 28)* Established 1769/1770, it provided benefits for disabled and time-expired officers and other ranks of the EIC/Indian Army and their widows but not children. Payments were 'ex gratia' and recipients subject to a means test. Last pensioner admitted c1886. In the OIOC Reading Room there is an index to officers' widows admitted to pension in the UK between 1769-1886, giving widow's date of admission and date of death. Fund registers, L/AG/23/2; Payment books, officers L/AG/21/10, other ranks L/AG/35/50-54, L/AG/21/45.

Madras Almanac *(pp10, 27)* Title from 1800 to 1859 of the annual directory for Madras City and Presidency. In 1799 it was called the Madras Register, from 1860 to 61 the New Madras Almanac and from 1862 to 1935 the Asylum Press Almanac. From the beginning it was printed and published at the Asylum Press, Madras, for the benefit of the Military Male Orphan Asylum. The OIOC Reading Room holds a complete set of these directories except for the years 1801-02 and 1804-10.

Madras Civil Fund *(p12)* *see* Bengal, Madras and Bombay Civil Funds.

Madras Medical Fund *(p24)* Established 1807, closed down 1870, it provided benefits for the widows and children of medical officers of the Madras Army. Its records at IOR are mainly mid-19th century onwards: Fund registers, L/AG/23/9; Payment books, L/AG/21/29.

Madras Military Fund *(pp18, 24, 28)* Established 1808, closed to new subscribers 1862, it provided benefits for the widows and children of regular officers and chaplains of the Madras Army – optional for Madras medical officers up to 1847. L/AG/23/10/1-2 comprise complete rolls of subscribers and their wives and children giving subscriber's dates of birth, marriage and death, wife's dates of birth and remarriage/death, children's dates of birth and daughters' dates of marriage/death – an edited transcript in one volume is available in the OIOC Reading Room. Fund registers, L/AG/23/10; Payment books, L/AG/21/32.

Magistrates and Collectors *(pp10-14)* Administrative titles used in the Regulation Provinces. For most of the period 1858-1947 the normal Indian Civil Service ranks in the Regulation Provinces (apart from Madras and Bombay) were, in ascending order: Assistant Magistrate and Collector, Joint Magistrate and Deputy Collector, Magistrate and Collector, Commissioner. In the Regulation Provinces members of the executive branch of the Provincial Civil Service held the rank of Deputy Magistrate and Deputy Collector. Magistrates exercised judicial functions in minor cases – the title Collector reflects their responsibility for revenue administration.

Matross *(pp21-22)* An inferior class of soldier in the EIC Artillery ranking below a Gunner.

Medical Annuities *(p24)* Additional pensions paid to officers of the Indian Medical Service. Medical annuities were contributory unlike the non-contributory ordinary Medical Service pensions. Payments of annuities are to be found in the series L/AG/21/15.

Military Fund Alternative name for the Lord Clive Fund *(q.v.)*.

Muster Rolls *(p21)* Annual nominal lists in a rough alphabetical order of the European private soldiers and NCOs in the East India Company's Bengal, Madras and Bombay Armies. From the early 19th century they provide information on a soldier's background.

Naik *(p29)* In the Indian Infantry an Indian non-commissioned officer equivalent to a Corporal in the British Army.

Nizamat Adalat *see* Sadr Nizamat Adalat.

Non-Commissioned Officers (NCOs) *(pp21-22, 31-32)* Army officers not appointed by a commission or warrant. In the British Army they held the ranks of Lance-Corporal, Corporal and Sergeant. *See also* Indian Non-Commissioned Officers, Warrant Officers.

Non-Effective Account These were the accounts between the Company, the Government of India and the Home Government, in connection with the cost of the services in India of the British Army, and later also Royal Air Force personnel. On rare occasions, payments were made for the use of Royal Navy and Royal Marine personnel.

Non-Regulation Province *(pp10-18)* An Indian province exempted from the operation of the Indian Government regulations and governed instead by a Commission under the direct authority of the Governor-General in Council, e.g. the Punjab after 1849. In the Non-Regulation Provinces officers of the EIC/Indian Army could hold posts in the top general administration – such posts were not open to them in the Regulation Provinces. The top executive grades in the Non-Regulation Provinces were, in ascending order: Assistant Commissioner, Deputy Commissioner, Commissioner, and Chief Commissioner or Lieutenant-Governor.

Order of British India *(p29)* Introduced by the East India Company in 1837 to reward its Indian commissioned officers for outstanding long and meritorious service. It consisted of two classes, recipients of the 1st Class receiving the title of Sardar Bahadur, recipients of the 2nd Class the title of Bahadur. Appointments to the 1st Class were made only from members of the 2nd Class. The Order ceased to be conferred in 1947.

Order of the Indian Empire, The Most Eminent *(p53)* Founded in Dec 1877 as a junior order to that of the Star of India. Originally it had only one class, that of Companion (CIE), but from 1887 it consisted of three classes: Companion (CIE),

Knight Commander (KCIE), and Knight Grand Commander (GCIE). For correspondence regarding the award and statements of service of recipients *see* the series L/P&S/15.

Order of Merit. Original name for the Indian Order of Merit.

Order of the Star of India, The Most Exalted *(p53)* Founded in 1861 as a reward for distinguished service in India. It consisted of three classes: Companion (CSI), Knight Commander (KCSI), and Knight Grand Commander (GCSI). For correspondence regarding the award and statements of service of recipients *see* the series L/P&S/15.

Ordnance Department *(pp15-22)* Name given to the department(s) of the EIC/Indian Army responsible for supplying ordnance (arms and ammunition). It became the Indian Army Ordnance Department, 1884, and the Indian Army Ordnance Corps, 1922.

Pembroke House *(p8)* Lunatic asylum in Hackney, East London (1818-1870) which looked after former employees of the East India Company – civil, military, marine – who were certified insane while in India. Patients were either subsidised by the Company or, if their income was above a certain level, were obliged to pay their own fees. In 1870 the patients were re-housed in a new institution, the Royal Indian Asylum in Ealing, West London, under direct India Office control – this institution was closed down in 1892.

Pilot Services *(p37)* By far the most important pilot service in India was the Bengal Pilot Service which was responsible for guiding sea-going ships up the Hooghly river from the Sandheads to Calcutta, and vice versa. The Hooghly, owing to its numerous shoals and shifting quicksands, presented special difficulties for navigators.

Pleader *(p41)* The equivalent in an Indian High Court of a barrister in England.

Poplar Pension Fund *(p39)* Provided benefits for disabled or otherwise unfit officers and seamen of the East India Company's Mercantile Marine, their widows and children. So-called because it originally came into existence to finance the upkeep of the Company's hospital-cum-almshouse established at Poplar in East London in 1627: Fund registers, mainly L/MAR/C/789-840, indexed at L/MAR/C/785-786: Payment books, mainly L/AG/21/7.

Preventive Officer *(pp13-14)* An officer of the Indian Customs Service employed in the suppression of smuggling.

Private *(pp21-22, 31-32)* Ordinary soldier in the British Infantry equivalent to a Sepoy in the Indian Infantry and a Sowar in the Indian Cavalry.

Provincial Civil Service *(pp13-14)* From 1892 the name given to the upper echelon of the Uncovenanted Civil Service (*q.v.*). Members of the service held the higher uncovenanted posts of Deputy Magistrate/Deputy Collector in the Executive Branch and of Subordinate Judge in the Judicial Branch. They were members of the domiciled Indian community and were recruited from the province in which they subsequently served. Members of the Provincial Civil Service are recorded in both the official Histories of Services (V/12) and Civil Lists (V/13).

Public Works Department *(pp10-22)* Government department responsible for buildings and roads, irrigation and railways. The history of Public Works organisation in India is quite complex (see *The Imperial Gazetteer of India*, 1908, Vol 4 pp 307-24). Military works originally formed a branch of the Government of India Public Works Department but during the latter half of the 19th century they were gradually detached from PWD control and in 1899 became fully part of the Indian Army organisation under the new title of Military Works Service.

Regular Officer *(pp15-18, 29)* In the Indian Army an officer holding the King's or Queen's commission. Until c1918 the regular officer corps of the Indian Army was almost entirely European but from 1918 onwards a small number of King's commissions were granted annually to Sandhurst trained Asian cadets and during World War II the number of Asians receiving such commissions greatly increased.

Regular Widows' and Elders' Widows' Funds *(p6)* Established 1816, it provided benefits for the widows and children of staff of the East India Company's Home Civil Service in London. Closed to new subscribers 1862. Established clerks contributed to the Regular Widows' Fund: the Elders' Widows' (or Extra) Fund was compulsory for established Elders (*q.v.*), doorkeepers, porters and warehousemen, and optional for non-established staff (including writers and extra clerks): Fund registers, L/AG/23/3A; Payment books, L/AG/21/23.

Regulation Province *(pp10-12)* An Indian province governed according to the existing regulations, as opposed to a Non-Regulation Province. The Regulation Provinces were the older provinces which had enjoyed a long period of settled administration, e.g. Bengal, Madras, Bombay. In the Regulation Provinces (Madras and Bombay excepted), for most of the period after 1858, the ICS executive grades (in ascending order) were Assistant Magistrate and Collector, Joint Magistrate and Deputy Collector, Magistrate and Collector, Commissioner, Lieutenant-Governor or Governor.

Ressaidar *(p29)* A rank of Indian cavalry officer intermediate between Jemadar and Risaldar. In April 1921 the rank of Ressaidar was abolished, all existing Ressaidars being regraded as Risaldars.

Risaldar *(p29)* A rank of Indian cavalry officer equivalent to a Subadar in the Indian Infantry. Until April 1921 it was intermediate between Ressaidar and Risaldar-Major, after that date between Jemadar and Risaldar-Major.

Risaldar-Major *(p29)* The most senior rank of Indian cavalry officer, equivalent to a Subadar-Major in the Indian Infantry.

Royal Warrant Pensions *(p20)* Non-contributory pensions awarded to widows and orphans of regular officers, warrant officers and chaplains of the Indian Army, Eligibility was limited to the families of those who entered Indian military service after 1881. Award of a pension was dependent on a means test. The pensions were first awarded from Indian revenues in April 1886 and appear to have superseded pensions from the Lord Clive Fund *(q.v.)* to which no new admissions were made after 1886. Records of the payments of Royal Warrant pensions are usually to be found in the books of the Indian Military Service Family Pension Fund (L/AG/21/35) unless the payee was in receipt of a second pension from another fund, eg the Indian Military Widows' and Orphans' Fund (L/AG/21/36) or the Madras Military Fund (L/AG/21/30) in which case the payment was recorded on the books of that fund.

Sadr Adalat *(p41)* A chief court of appeal from courts administering Hindu and Islamic Law. For the different types of Sadr Adalat *see below*.

Sadr Diwani Adalat *(p41)* Until 1862 the chief civil court of appeal from courts administering Hindu and Islamic Law. In 1862 the Sadr Adalats of Calcutta, Madras and Bombay were amalgamated with the Supreme Courts to form the High Courts.

Sadr Faujdari Adalat *(p41)* Until 1862 the chief criminal court of appeal in the Madras and Bombay Presidencies from courts administering Hindu and Islamic Law. In 1862 the Sadr Adalats of Calcutta, Madras and Bombay were amalgamated with the Supreme Courts to form the High Courts.

Sadr Nizamat Adalat *(p41)* Until 1862 the chief criminal court of appeal in the Bengal Presidency from courts administering Hindu and Islamic Law. In 1862 the Sadr Adalats of Calcutta, Madras and Bombay were amalgamated with the Supreme Courts to form the High Courts.

Senior Merchant *(pp10-12)* The first of the four classes into which the East India Company's civil servants were originally divided, the others being 2) Junior Merchant, 3) Factor and 4) Writer. As the title indicates it originally had a commercial significance, but it continued to be used as a rank in the Company's service long after the duties of the Company's officials had ceased to be primarily commercial – it last appears as a civil service rank in the East India Register in 1841.

Sepoy (p29) In the EIC/Indian Army an ordinary native infantryman equivalent to a Sowar in the Indian Cavalry.

Silladar *(p29)* An Indian cavalryman who provided his own arms and horse instead of having them supplied by Government. The Silladar system originated in the irregular regiments of native cavalry but was extended to the regular cavalry of the Bengal and Bombay Armies in 1861.

Sowar *(p29)* In the EIC/Indian Army an ordinary native cavalryman equivalent to a Sepoy in the Indian Infantry and to a Trooper in the British Cavalry.

Special Civil Services *(pp10-12)* Special departments of the Indian administration, e.g. the Indian Forest Service, Indian Police, Indian Political Service, etc, to be distinguished both from the Covenanted Civil Service and the Uncovenanted Civil Service. The top echelons of the special services were recruited in a variety of ways. The Indian Political Service was recruited partly from the HEICS/ICS, partly from officers of the EIC/Indian Army. The Indian Police in its earlier days included many officers of the Indian

Army but from 1893 onwards recruited its upper division mainly by an annual competitive examination held in the UK.

Staff Corps *(pp15-18)* A Staff Corps for the Bengal, Madras and Bombay Armies (i.e. the Indian Army) was set up in 1861. The Staff Corps was to provide officers for the native regiments, and for the staff and army departments, as also for civil and political appointments for which Indian Army officers might be eligible. Officers already in employ had the option of joining the Staff Corps or staying on under the old conditions. The Staff Corps therefore at least as far as post-1860 entrants were concerned was virtually synonymous with the Regular Officer Corps of the Indian Army and is not to be understood in the narrow sense of officers holding staff appointments. In 1903 in order to avoid confusion the designation 'Indian Staff Corps' as applied to officers on regimental duty was withdrawn and replaced by the more appropriate term 'Indian Army'.

Subadar *(p29)* A rank of Indian infantry officer intermediate between Jemadar and Subadar-Major, equivalent to a Captain in the British Army and to a Risaldar in the Indian Cavalry.

Subadar-Major *(p29)* The most senior rank of Indian infantry officer, equivalent to a Risaldar-Major in the Indian cavalry.

Sub-Conductor *(pp19-20)* The lower of the two Warrant Officer ranks in the EIC/Indian Army, the higher being that of Conductor. Sub-Conductors and Conductors worked mainly in the Ordnance, Commissariat and Public Works Departments. Before 1860 Sub-Conductors were recruited from NCOs of the Town Major's List/Effective Supernumeraries, after 1860 from NCOs of the Unattached List.

Subordinate Civil Service *(pp13-14)* Name given from 1892 to the lower echelon of the Uncovenanted Civil Service. Members of the Subordinate Civil Service held the posts of Tahsildar in the Executive Branch and Munsif in the Judicial Branch.

Superior Services *(pp10-18)* Collective name for the Indian Civil Service and the top echelons of the Special Civil Services, until the 1920s mainly recruited from British natural-born subjects in the UK.

Superior Services (India) Family Pension Fund (SSIFPF) *(p14)* Established in 1928, it provided

benefits for the widows and children of members of the Superior Services, India, other than the ICS: Family registers, L/AG/23/14; Payment books, mainly L/AG/21/33.

Supreme Courts *(p41)* Established at Calcutta, 1774, Madras 1801, Bombay 1823. They administered mainly English civil and criminal law. In 1862 the Supreme Courts were replaced by High Courts which combined the functions formerly exercised by the Supreme Courts and the Sadr Adalats *(q.v.)*.

Town Major's List *(pp19, 21)* Name given in the EIC Bengal and Bombay Armies to the select cadre of European NCOs who served extra-regimentally, mainly in the Ordnance, Commissariat and Public Works Departments. In the Madras Presidency they were known as Effective Supernumeraries. Recruited largely from NCOs of the Company's European Corps, and occasionally from NCOs of British Army regiments in India, they are recorded in the annual Muster Rolls of the Bengal, Madras and Bombay Armies (L/MIL/10,11,12). NCOs on the Town Major's List/Effective Supernumeraries were eligible for promotion to the warrant officer rank of Sub-Conductor. In 1859/60 the Town Major's List was replaced by the Unattached List.

Trooper *(pp21-22, 31-32)* An ordinary soldier in the British Cavalry equivalent to a Private in the Infantry and a Gunner in the Artillery.

Unattached List. Two distinct meanings:
(1) **Unattached List – NCOs – Indian Army** *(p21)*: name given after 1859 to the special cadre of European NCOs who served extra-regimentally in the Indian Army. They were employed mainly in the Ordnance, Commissariat and Public Works Departments but also in a number of minor departments and in various miscellaneous posts. The Unattached List replaced the former EIC Town Major's List/Effective Supernumeraries. NCOs on the Unattached List were, after 1859, recruited solely from NCOs of British Army regiments stationed in India and could be remanded to their parent regiments in cases of incompetence and/or misconduct. A soldier on the Unattached List only became fully part of the Indian Army if and when subsequently promoted to the warrant officer rank of Sub-Conductor.
(2) **Unattached List – Officers – Indian Army** *(p15)*: List of graduates of the Royal Military Academy, Sandhurst, granted commissions in the Indian Army but serving a probationary year

with a British Army regiment in India before joining the Indian Army proper. During their probationary year they were required to obtain a basic qualification in a vernacular language failing which their probation was extended by a further year. Lists of officers on the Unattached List are recorded in the quarterly Indian Army Lists.

Uncovenanted Civil Service *(pp13-14)* Name given to the lower echelon of the general civil service in India under both the East India Company and the Crown, to be distinguished both from the upper echelon or Covenanted Civil Service and from the Special Civil Services. The Uncovenanted Civil Service was recruited almost entirely from persons born in India, whether European, Eurasian or Asian. In 1892 the Uncovenanted Civil Service was further subdivided into an upper branch or Provincial Civil Service and a lower branch or Subordinate Civil Service.

Viceroy's Commissioned Officers (VCOs) *(p29)* Name given after 1858 to native officers of the Indian Army, so-called because they received their commissions from the Viceroy, not from the Monarch. *See also* Indian Commissioned Officers.

Voluntary Aid Detachments (VADs) *(p26)* Special nursing service recruited from volunteers in the UK during World War II, for service with the British armed forces overseas.

Volunteer Force – India *see* Indian Volunteer Force.

Warehouses *(p6)* The East India Company owned or rented several large warehouses in the City of London and vicinity for the storage of its trade goods. For a note on these warehouses and the people who worked in them *see* M I Moir, *Guide to the India Office Records*, p 40.

Warrant Officers *(pp19-20)* Officers appointed by warrant. In the EIC/Indian Army they held the ranks of Sub-Conductor and Conductor and were intermediate in rank between Non-Commissioned Officers and Departmental Officers. In addition, from 1882 a small number of British Army warrant officers with the rank of Sergeant-Major or Quarter Master Sergeant were appointed to non-departmental posts in the Indian Army.

Women's Auxiliary Corps – India (WAC(I)) and **Burma (WAC(B))** *(p26)* Established 1942. Non-combatant corps providing support services for the Indian Army and Burma Army in World War II. The equivalent of the Auxiliary Territorial Service (ATS) in the UK.

Writer *(pp6-8, 10-14, 46-49)* Two distinct meanings:
(1) The lowest of the four classes into which the East India Company's civil servants were divided, the others being 1) Senior Merchant, 2) Junior Merchant, 3) Factor. The term reflects the fact that in the early years of the Company copying and book-keeping comprised the greater part of a writer's duties but it continued to be used as a rank in the Company's service long after the duties of the Company's officials had ceased to be primarily commercial – it last appears as a civil service rank in the East India Register in 1841.
(2) A copying clerk in an office. For copying clerks employed at East India House in London *see* p6. As regards India several thousand copying clerks were employed by the Central, Provincial and District authorities but their individual names are rarely recorded in the official records.

Writers' Petitions *(p10)* Appointment papers of the East India Company's young civil servants, giving details of parentage and educational attainment (1749-1805): *see* J/1/1-19. This series is incomplete. It is continued by the 'Committee of College References and Papers' (1806-56): *see* J/1/21-90. *See also* East India College.

Zillah. Alternative name for an Indian District.

Ecclesiastical Returns Areas

Listed below are the districts, major princely states, and other main towns in each Ecclesiastical Returns area. Place names are taken from the revised (1931) atlas of the *Imperial Gazetteer of India.* Changes were made in administrative boundaries from time to time, so that events in 'border' districts should sometimes be sought in adjoining areas. For example, before 1865 (and sometimes even afterwards) events in Nagpur and Kamptee will be found in the Madras rather than Bengal returns. Events in Hyderabad and Mysore should also be checked in both the Bombay and Bengal indexes. Events in Baluchistan (Quetta) are sometimes found in the Bombay indexes. Burma returns were indexed separately after 1937. For map see back cover.

BENGAL Returns (IOR/N/1)

Bengal

Districts: Bakarganj, Bankura, Birbhum, Bogra, Burdwan, Calcutta, Chittagong, Chittagong Hill Tracts, Dacca, Darjeeling, Dinajpur, Faridpur, Hooghly, Howrah, Jalpaiguri, Jessore, Khulna, Malda, Midnapore, Murshidabad, Mymensingh, Nadia, Noakhali, Pabna, Rajshahi, Rangpur, Tippera, Twenty-four Parganas
Other main towns: Alipur, Asansol, Barisal, Barrackpore, Berhampur, Chinsurah, Comilla, Dum Dum, English Bazar, Kalimpong, Khargpur, Kidderpore, Krishnagar, Rampur Boalia, Raniganj, Serampore, Suri

Bihar

Districts: Bhagalpur, Champaran, Darbhanga, Gaya, Hazaribagh, Manbhum, Monghyr, Muzaffarpur, Palamau, Patna, Purnea, Ranchi, Santal Parganas, Saran, Shahabad, Singhbhum
Other main towns: Arrah, Chaibassa, Chapra, Daltonganj, Dinapore, Dumka, Jamalpur, Jamshedpur, Laheria Serai, Motihari, Purulia

Assam

Districts: Balipara, Cachar, Darrang, Garo Hills, Goalpara, Kamrup, Lakhimpur, Lushai Hills, Naga Hills, Nowgong, Sadiya, Sibsagar, Sylhet
Major states: Khasi and Jaintia Hills, Manipur
Other main towns: Aijal, Charduar, Dhubri, Dibrugarh, Gauhati, Imphal, Jorhat, Kohima, Shillong, Silchar, Tezpur, Tura

United Provinces

Districts: Agra, Aligarh, Allahabad, Almora, Azamgarh, Bahraich, Ballia, Banda, Bara Banki, Bareilly, Basti, Benares, Bijnor, Budaun, Bulandshahr, Cawnpore, Dehra Dun, Etah, Etawah, Farrukhabad, Fatehpur, Fyzabad, Garhwal, Ghazipur, Gonda, Gorakhpur, Hamirpur, Hardoi, Jalaun, Jaunpur, Jhansi, Kheri, Lucknow, Mainpuri, Meerut, Mirzapur, Moradabad, Muttra, Muzaffarnagar, Naini Tal, Partabgarh, Pilibhit, Rae Bareli, Saharanpur, Shahjahanpur, Sitapur, Sultanpur, Tehri, Unao
Other main towns: Bela, Chakrata, Chunar, Landour, Mussoorie, Nawabganj, Pauri, Ranikhet, Roorkee

Punjab

Districts: Ambala, Amritsar, Attock, Dera Ghazi Khan, Ferozepore, Gujranwala, Gujrat, Gurdaspur, Gurgaon, Hissar, Hoshiarpur, Jhang, Jhelum, Jullundur, Kangra, Karnal, Lahore, Ludhiana, Lyallpur, Mianwali, Montgomery, Multan, Muzaffargarh, Rawalpindi, Rohtak, Shahpur, Shekhupura,. Sialkot, Simla
Other main towns: Campbellpore, Dagshai, Dalhousie, Dharmsala, Jutogh, Kalka, Kasauli, Kotkhai, Murree, Sargodha, Subathu

Delhi

Central Provinces

Districts: Akola, Amraoti, Balaghat, Betul, Bhandara, Bilaspur, Buldana, Chanda, Chhindwara, Drug, Hoshangabad, Jubbulpore, Mandla, Nagpur, Nimar, Raipur, Saugor, Wardha, Yeotmal
Other main towns: Kamptee, Khandwa, Narsinghpur, Pachmarhi, Seoni

Orissa

Districts: Angul, Balasore, Cuttack, Ganjam, Khondmals, Koraput, Puri, Sambalpur
Other main towns: Berhampur, Chatrapur

North West Frontier Province

Districts: Bannu, Dera Ismail Khan, Hazara, Kohat, Peshawar

Major states: Chitral, Dir, Swat, Waziristan
Other main towns: Abbottabad, Landi Kotal,
Nowshera, Parachinar, Razmak, Risalpur, Thal,
Wana

Baluchistan
Districts: Chagai, Loralai, Quetta-Pishin, Sibi,
Zhob
States: Kalat, Las Bela
Other main towns: Bela, Quetta

Rajputana
Major states: Alwar, Bharatpur, Bikaner, Jaipur,
Jaisalmer, Jodhpur, Kotah, Udaipur
District: Ajmer-Merwara
Other main towns: Ajmer, Nasirabad

Punjab States
Major states: Bahawalpur, Chamba, Jind,
Kapurthala, Khairpur, Mandi, Nabha, Patiala,
Tehri-Garhwal

Central India
Major states: Bhopal, Dhar, Indore, Orchha,
Panna, Rewa
Other main towns: Manpur, Mhow, Neemuch,
Nowgong

Gwalior
States: Benares, Gwalior, Rampur
Other main towns: Lashkar, Mandasor, Ujjain

Eastern States
Major states: Bastar, Cooch Behar, Kalahandi,
Keonjhar, Mayurbhanj, Patna, Surguja, Tripura

Jammu and Kashmir
Main towns: Gilgit, Jammu, Leh, Srinagar

Gilgit
Main town: Chilas

Andaman and Nicobar Islands
Main towns: Nancowry, Port Blair

Burma
Main districts: Akyab, Amherst, Bassein, Bhamo,
Hanthawaddy, Kyaukpyu, Mandalay, Meiktila
Mergui, Minbu, Myitkyina, Pakokku, Pegu, Prome,
Rangoon, Salween, Sandoway, Shwebo, Tavoy,
Thayetmyo, Toungoo, Yamethin
Major state: Karenni
Other main towns: Martaban, Moulmein, Sagaing,
Syriam

MADRAS Returns (IOR/N/2)
Madras
Districts: Anantapur, North Arcot, South Arcot,
Bellary, Chingleput, Chittoor, Coimbatore,
Cuddapah, East Godavari, West Godavari, Guntur,
South Kanara, Kistna, Kurnool, Madras, Madura,
Malabar, Nellore, Nilgiri, Ramnad, Salem, Tanjore,
Tinnevelly, Trichinopoly, Vizagapatam
Other main towns: Calicut, Cocanada, Cochin,
Coonoor, Cuddalore, Ellore, Mangalore,
Masulipatam, Ootacamund, Saidapet, Tuticorin,
Vellore, Wellington

Madras States
States: Cochin, Pudukkottai, Travancore
Main towns: Alleppey, Ernakulam, Trivandrum

Hyderabad
Main towns: Aurangabad, Bolarum, Chadarghat,
Gulbarga, Hyderabad, Mahbubnagar, Nizamabad,
Raichur, Secunderabad, Warangal

Mysore
States: Banganapalle, Mysore, Sandur
Districts: North Coorg, South Coorg
Main towns: Bangalore, Chikmagalur, Chitaldrug,
Hassan, Kolar, Mandya, Mercara, Mysore,
Shimoga, Tumkur

BOMBAY Returns (IOR/N/3)
Bombay
Districts: Ahmadabad, Ahmadnagar, Belgaum,
Bijapur, Bombay, Broach and Panch Mahals,
Dharwar, Kaira, North Kanara, East Khandesh,
West Khandesh, Kolaba, Nasik, Poona, Ratnagiri,
Satara, Sholapur, Surat, Thana
Other main towns: Alibag, Dhulia, Godhra,
Jalgaon, Karwar, Kirkee

Sind
Districts: Dadu, Hyderabad, Karachi, Larkana,
Nawabshah, Sukkur, Thar Parkar, Upper Sind
Frontier
Other main towns: Jacobabad, Mirpur Khas,
Shikarpur

Baroda, Gujarat and Western India States
Major states: Baroda, Bhavnagar, Cutch, Gondal,
Junagadh, Nawanagar, Rajpipla
Other main towns: Amreli, Bhuj, Cambay,
Navsari, Rajkot, Wadhwan

Kolhapur and Deccan States
Major states: Janjira, Kolhapur, Sangli, Sawantwadi